Women on Heroin

A Volume in the
Crime, Law, and Deviance
Series

Women on Heroin

Marsha Rosenbaum

Rutgers University Press
New Brunswick, New Jersey

Second Printing, 1985

Library of Congress Cataloging in Publication Data

Rosenbaum, Marsha, 1948–
    Women on heroin.

    Bibliography: p.
    Includes index.
    1. Heroin habit.   2. Women—Mental health.
I. Title.   [DNLM: 1. Heroin addiction.   2. Women.
WM 288 R813w]
RC568.H4R67   362.2'93'088042   80-29566
ISBN 0-8135-0921-1
ISBN 0-8135-0946-7 (pbk.)

A section of Chapter 6 is reprinted from "Difficulties in Taking Care of Business: Women Addicts as Mothers," *American Journal of Drug and Alcohol Abuse* 6 (1979) 431–446, by courtesy of Marcel Dekker, Inc.

For John

Contents

Acknowledgments

Several individuals helped me complete this book. John Irwin acted as a 24-hour-a-day colleague who listened to every aspect of data collection and analysis while supporting me through writing pains and several revisions. He added sociological insight and personal wisdom to the analysis, read each chapter, and helped to take care of business at home so that I could devote full attention to this project. Sheigla Murphy, my research assistant and "crime partner," conducted a substantial portion of the interviews, provided assistance in the literature review, spent many hours discussing the data, and was always available as a sounding board to my emergent (and often tortured) analysis. She was also responsible for compiling the glossary in Appendix IV. Sharon Harsha, project secretary, transcribed over 90 interviews, and typed, edited, and criticized each chapter.

Anselm Strauss, Leonard Schatzman, and Troy Duster helped discover the basic social process of this analysis: narrowing options. They continually forced me to translate substance into theory and process and gave consistent encouragement while pushing me analytically. Michael Agar, Howard Becker, Diane Beeson, Herbert Blumer, and David Greenberg read the entire manuscript and made thoughtful and valuable comments that led to the final draft. Their encouragement at the book stage of this endeavor was most appreciated.

Several colleagues read and commented on portions of the manuscript: Pat Biernacki, Robert Broadhead, Jennifer James, and especially Dan Waldorf. Other individuals gave hours of verbal assistance: Stephanie Berman, Dean Gerstein, Barney Glaser, David Matza, and Jerry Skolnick. Lisa Fraiberg, Adelle Lopez, and Sydelle Rosenbaum edited and proofed portions of the manuscript.

The Institute for Scientific Analysis (especially Dorothy Miller, Bruce Jones, and Setsu Ota-Gee) provided a conducive working environment. Al Richmond read and edited the entire manuscript, and Cassandra Curtiss-Zimmerman gave excellent secretarial assistance throughout the project. Les Morgan aided Sheigla Murphy in preparing tables and demographic statistics.

The National Institute on Drug Abuse funded the project in its entirety. Louise Richards, the project officer, was always available for advice and counseling and gave enthusiastic support; without her and NIDA, this project may not have been completed.

Marlie Wasserman at Rutgers University Press gave editorial direction and was extremely encouraging. Leslie Mitchner and Marilyn Buckingham did a thorough and excellent job editing.

As a mother, I had to make special arrangements in order to complete this book. My parents, Sydelle and Ed Rosenbaum, gave emotional and financial support and provided my daughter, Anne, with care and comfort, as did my sister, Ellen Rosenbaum, my stepdaughters, Jenny and Katy Irwin, and Gladys Jefferson, Annie's day-care mother.

Finally and most important are the 100 women who shared their stories with me. They provided the data or, put more appropriately, the descriptions and details of their experience. Without the accounts of these women who struggle daily with the burden of addiction, this project would have been impossible.

Women on Heroin

CHAPTER ONE

Introduction

Prior to 1914, drug addiction was not defined as a crime, and addiction was most often supported by physicians' prescriptions. The recipients of most of these prescriptions were women diagnosed by their physicians as weak, fragile, and in need of medical treatments such as opiates.[1] Shortly after the turn of the century, women addicts outnumbered men by a ratio of two to one.[2] After the passage of the Harrison Act, which radically altered prescription practices, the incidence of women's addiction to opiates dropped dramatically. When opiate addiction became illegal, it became a male form of deviance, and even with the general rise of addiction following World War II, women's rates did not increase as significantly as men's.[3] Over the last decade, however, women's participation in the world of heroin has increased significantly. In 1968 men addicts outnumbered women by a margin of five to one; ten years later that ratio had been reduced to three to one, and all indications point to a further narrowing between the two figures.[4]

It is not surprising that until recently women have not been prominent in the world of heroin. The nature of addiction—the rough, almost frenzied street life of the addict—runs counter to women's traditional involvement in domestic life as wives and mothers. And yet in the last decade or two, as with other "male" activities, women have entered the heroin world. Who are these women? What is the nature of their experience in the world of illegal opiates? How do they fare in the heroin life? In the next few pages I look at what others have concluded about women addicts in an attempt to answer my own questions.

The Woman Addict: What We Know about Her

Most of what is known about women addicts is in the medical realm and centers on reproductive issues. In this extensive literature, the unborn fetus or withdrawing neonate has been the focus of attention,[5] although social science-oriented medical research has given some attention to the mother-child unit in reproductive issues.[6] A second large area of research has focused on epidemiological and comparative issues in women's addiction. Researchers who have gathered both demographic and epidemiological data have compared women addicts with men,[7] among races,[8] through time,[9] and with other kinds of drug users;[10] criminality has been another area of study.[11] The treatment experience and behavior of the woman addict have also been explored.[12] Finally, there have been life-history/career studies of women addicts as subsets of larger mixed populations[13] and a notable biography.[14] The following section summarizes the substantive contributions of this literature.

The background of the woman addict has been analyzed from primarily a psychiatric perspective: She often comes from a home that is disrupted and disruptive and experiences a disproportionate amount of sexual as well as other kinds of violence. The woman addict has difficulty getting along with her mother and tends to have a better relationship with her father; she is often met, however, with violence and sexual advances by her stepfather. It has been argued in much of the psychiatric literature that she is immature and sexually confused, feels unloved, and often becomes pregnant both as an act of defiance and in an attempt to be loved.

Demographic data indicate that women's drug use prior to heroin addiction has changed, particularly with regard to white women. Before 1965, addiction was often iatrogenic (the result of medical treatment), whereas the hippie movement introduced the more widespread use of marijuana prior to addiction. Although white women had become addicted to heroin at a later age than men or black women (as a function of their medical entree into addiction) and still tend to begin heroin use later than blacks or men, the age of entree dropped with the hippie movement.

There is disagreement over many of the findings but particularly, over the question of how women are initiated into heroin use. Older research pointed to spousal introduction as the most common mode of entree: The woman was seen as passive and subject to the whims of her man. Newer studies indicate that women, like men, begin to use heroin in mixed social groups and for such reasons as curiosity, sociability, and the like. Even in social groups, women tend to be connected with a man who is also using heroin (whereas the reverse is not so).

Reasons for heroin use by women fall into three basic categories: personality characteristics, psychological reinforcement, and social reinforcement.[15] Some researchers argue that using heroin is equivalent to the passive woman asserting her independence and venting her aggressions.[16] The woman addict continues to use heroin because she enjoys the thrill or high of the drug; she also gains the acceptance of a social group of users,[17] something she lacked from other sources.

Initial and subsequent short-range heroin use is generally not costly to the woman, but ultimately she must begin to support her heroin habit and generally resorts to illegal means to do so. It has been widely documented that prostitution often accompanies addiction in women. Some researchers make the claim that due to the ease with which women can prostitute themselves, they can maintain a habit for longer periods of time than men. There are numerous other ways, however, that addicted women support a heroin habit; it has been found that in addition to prostitution, they are involved in crimes against property but not often against persons. They also participate, though to a lesser extent, in such crimes as shoplifting and selling drugs. The mode of work and the way in which it is carried out reflect the woman's sex role orientation. Interestingly enough, the woman addict is seen as deviant because she violates societal norms about what is proper and legal for women, but her own perspective remains traditional.[18] In fact, she exploits the female role in her work and, in many ways, identifies with this role but is ambivalent about her own deviation. Several researchers claim that immersion in the heroin lifestyle "has profound negative effects on women's self-concepts."[19]

The woman addict comes to the attention of correctional, medical, and rehabilitative institutions when she is arrested, gives birth, or seeks treatment for withdrawal. In terms of correction, although women addicts tend to be arrested frequently, they serve shorter sentences than men who are addicts. However, they often become readdicted after incarceration, commit crimes, recidivate, and serve many sentences. Black women, like black men, tend to have more arrests prior to their addiction than do whites, who enter the criminal justice system after having become addicted. Race and social class have a bearing on imprisonment: Those women who are disadvantaged at the outset tend to spend more time in prison and thus risk further alienation and isolation.

In the area of reproduction, the unborn fetus and addicted neonate have been studied extensively by the medical profession, which has found that the unborn fetus often becomes addicted in utero and goes through withdrawal at the time of birth but can be treated. But even if the infant is not born addicted, there are medical problems: Babies born to addicted mothers and impoverished women in general often have low birth weight and are usually in poor health. The pregnant addict herself often suffers from toxemia and risks losing the baby if she attempts withdrawal. (There is little consensus as to whether attempting withdrawal during pregnancy or withdrawing the newborn is more dangerous.) Although the addicted mother is almost peripheral (relative to the child) in medical research on addiction in women, she is nonetheless held responsible for what has been depicted (quite rightfully) as the horror of creating newborn addiction.

As in studies of male addicts, most of the women studied have been institutionalized; treatment has, in fact, been one of the central aspects in studying women addicts. Through research on women in treatment, the woman addict has come to be seen as more pathological than her male counterpart. She scores higher on tests of pathology, is said to be insecure, frightened, anxious, confused about her role and status in society, hostile, rebellious, without motivation, manipulative, selfish, and aggressive! Women addicts are, it is claimed, more difficult, therefore, to treat, and their drop-out rates reflect this difficulty, as they are much higher than men's. The results of treatment—relapse, recidivism, or cure—have been a major concern to researchers studying women in treatment. If women exhibit behavioral problems during treatment, thereby lessening the impact of the rehabilitative process, several feminist-oriented researchers assert that they have found the treatment experience to be inherently conflictive for women. While the ideology of women's treatment programs mirrors the notion of women's proper societal roles as mothers, wives, and homemakers, there are no childcare provisions for the addict-mother during her stay in treatment.

What's Missing?

Research on the woman addict has been neither fair nor exceedingly accurate nor objective in its portrayal. She has been depicted as more deviant than her male counterpart—psychologically as well as socially—yet the research upon which these findings are based has been spotty. One study often builds upon another in what is considered to be the information bank about women addicts, with the result that a systematic, processual investigation of the woman addict's experience and career has been sorely missed.

This book fills the gap in existing substantive knowledge about women addicts. It is an analysis of women and their careers in the (male) world of addiction. Is the female addict a liberated woman who breaks through sexual barriers and functions alongside men in the heroin world? Or is she doubly oppressed and exploited as an addict and a woman?

In order to fully comprehend the draw of the heroin world, it is necessary to understand the dynamics of entree into addiction. It is also necessary to explore the heroin world itself in order to understand the progressive inundation that makes outside social life nearly impossible. And what of this outside social life? Jobs are relinquished; so are husbands, often parents. But what happens to the children? Where do they fit in? Or out? An increased concern for the welfare of children, as evidenced by the declaration of the International Year of the Child in 1979, renders the study of the heroin-addicted mother indispensable.

Women's participation in the criminal world has increased along with heroin addiction; there is a great deal of overlap between women criminals and women addicts. What is the nature of their involvement in crime? Is it serious career crime or spontaneous capers? And again, what is the impact on the woman's domestic life when she is out "hustling" or "doing time"?

The last decade has seen an increase in size and number of treatment facilities that purport to serve the addict's needs; how do women fare in these facilities? If they are useful and helpful, action should be taken to expand facilities; if they are counterproductive, the reasons why should be explored and adjustments made accordingly. Otherwise, these facilities are simply a misuse of monies—private or public.

Above all, before any proposal is made or any action taken, it is imperative to have a complete understanding of how all the parts fit: how the woman enters the heroin world; why she stays; how she becomes addicted and ultimately supports herself; what happens to the life she lived prior to heroin—including, and especially, children and family but also occupational activities; how she fares in the criminal justice system and treatment facilities; most importantly, what it means to be a woman in this arena.

In order to address these issues in women's addiction, I examine the "career" of the woman addict; more specifically, I analyze the experience of the woman addict in terms of a career of narrowing options.

Theoretical Framework and Methodology

As already indicated, the literature available on women addicts is open to question, which is due largely to the use of narrow theoretical frameworks focusing on only psychological and psychiatric issues while ignoring the social and cultural context in which addiction arises and is maintained. A second problem is the reliance on quantitative methods that (1) often fail to examine meaning, motivation, and coping strategies of the addict and (2) contribute little to understanding the problem of addiction from the perspective of the addict.

This research was planned on the fundamental assumption that the definitions, meanings, and categories employed by actors themselves are important factors in structuring their activities. All social scientific theories, no matter how abstract, are built upon this common sense phenomenon. As Alfred Schutz has argued:

> the facts, events and data before the social scientist are of an entirely different structure. His observational field, the social world, is not essentially structureless. It has a particular meaning and relevance structure for the human beings living and acting therein. They have preselected and pre-interpreted this world by a series of common sense constructs of the reality of daily life and it is these thought objects which determine their behavior, define the goal of their action, the means available for attaining them—in brief, which enable them to find their bearings within their natural and socio-cultural environment and to come to terms with it. The thought objects constructed by the social scientists refer to and are founded upon the thought objects constructed by common sense thought of man living his everyday life among his fellow men. Thus, the constructs used by the social scientists are, so to speak, constructs of the second degree, namely, constructs of the constructs made by the actors on the social scene, whose behavior the scientist observes and tries to explain in accordance with the procedural rules of his science.[20]

The methodology of this project was guided by a combination of the philosophy of phenomenology and the theoretical perspective of symbolic interactionism. The individual's perspective on his/her social world is central to his/her experiences, and in order to understand an individual's experience, the phenomenologist maintains that this perspective must be understood. The perspective of symbolic interactionism as introduced by George Herbert Mead[21] and elaborated by Herbert Blumer[22] maintains that one interacts with the environment and others symbolically through language and builds a world through common definitions. It is through interaction that a social world, a society, emerges. Also central to symbolic interactionism are the concepts of identity and process. In order to understand any social phenomenon, one must understand the definitions and patterns of interaction that are operative.

The concept of career as initially introduced by the Chicago School in sociology, and elaborated by such theoreticians as Howard Becker, Erving Goffman, and Edwin Lemert, is my general theoretical framework. The career concept is especially useful because it is processual, focuses on identity, and has been purged of its overtones of success or failure. As Goffman says:

> Traditionally, the term *career* has been reserved for those who expect to enjoy the rises laid out within a respectable profession. The term is coming to be used, however, in a broadened sense to refer to any social strand of any person's course through life. The perspective of natural history is taken: unique outcomes are neglected in favor of such changes over time as are basic and common to the members of a social category, although occurring independently to each of them. Such a career is not a thing that can be brilliant or disappointing; it can no more be a success than a failure.[23]

The career concept makes it possible to look processually, sequentially, temporally, social psychologically, and (as much as possible), nonjudgmentally at the individual's experience with drugs (or any other type of career). Unlike more traditional sociological and psychological frameworks, it approaches drug-related activities primarily from the perspective of the user. A symbolic interactionist and phenomenologist subscribes to the belief that life should be understood as the actor sees it. However, it is also necessary to strike a compromise methodologically and combine the reports of informants with objective social science. The grounded theory method allows this combination in both collecting and analyzing data. This method, introduced by Glaser and Strauss[24] and elaborated by Glaser,[25] is based on the idea that data should be collected and analyzed so that the basic social, social-psychological, and structural processes inherent in the phenomena emerge during data gathering. Data are initially collected with few preconceived notions about the nature of the phenomena under study. After a small amount of data is collected, the process of theoretical sampling takes over. As the researcher begins to see patterns taking shape, s/he chooses the sample according to gaps in the data. This process continues until all possibilities have been exhausted and a saturation point reached. While collecting data, the researcher continually makes theoretical, analytical, and methodological notes that guide her/him through the data-gathering stage and into analysis.[26] Interviews are coded according to the salient categories that are emergent. The combination of notes and codes makes up memos, which are then organized into appropriate categories; eventually, the researcher builds a memo bank, the basis for the final analysis.

My sample consisted of 100 women addicts; 95 resided in the San Francisco Bay Area and 5 in New York City. The population was split nearly equally between white (43 percent) and black (38 percent) women; there were also 14 Latinas, 1 Asian, 1 native American, and 3 Filipinos. The ages of the women ranged from 20 to 53, with a median of 28. The exact composition of the addict population is unknown: There is no central registry or census. However, those institutions that treat addicts have census data limited to one locale and time period. I used a combination of treatment facilities' intake statistics and the reports of prior studies to get a rough determination of proper racial/ethnic proportions. Therefore, although I do not claim representativeness in the strict statistical sense, my sample does reflect the current population of women heroin addicts in San Francisco.

This project could be considered a street study because the women sampled were primarily active, uninstitutionalized heroin users. The sample was procured by posting notices in high drug-using areas, city prison, and a variety of treatment facilities. The snowball method was also used to locate members of neighborhood worlds and friendship groups.

There are inherent methodological problems with collecting data on a deviant population. Due to the risk of exposure, it might seem that heroin addicts would be reticent to talk in depth with researchers. Both the project personnel and I were surprised to learn, however, that rapport came easily, possibly because we were women talking openly with women, and we had no trouble getting long, indepth, frank accounts of the women's lives and especially of their experience with drugs.

All interviews were completely voluntary. They were conducted primarily in our own interviewing office and women's homes (with the exception of 17 that were done in city prison). A $20 remuneration was awarded the respondents. The depth-interview/life-history method was used as a primary data collection tool. The interviews took between two and three hours and touched on all aspects of the women's lives, with a focus on their drug-using careers; demographic statistics were also collected.

The project personnel and I also did field work in San Francisco, where we spent time talking with addicts in high drug-using areas while publicizing our project. We visited some of the women in their homes and accompanied our addicted associates on their rounds in their communities, including treatment facilities, "scoring" places, and "shooting galleries."[27]

A Career of Narrowing Options

In analyzing the career of the woman addict, I found that her career is inverted. Heroin expands her life options in the initial stages, and that is the essence of its social attraction. Yet with progressively further immersion in the heroin world, the social, psychological, and physiological exigencies of heroin use create an option "funnel" for the woman addict. Through this funnel the addict's life options are gradually reduced until she is functionally incarcerated in an invisible prison. Ultimately, the woman addict is locked into the heroin life and locked out of the conventional world.

This narrowing of options is the primary process in the woman addict's career. Typically, she begins life with a status of relatively reduced options and then drifts into the heroin world; the conditions associated with this life steadily, almost inevitably, narrow her options further. Ultimately, her reduced options outside the heroin world become a rationale for continued drug use and an even further immersion in deviance. The social processes, conditions, and variables that trigger and sustain this narrowing career are the focus of analysis in this book.

In order to begin an analysis of the woman addict's career, the structure of the heroin world must be detailed. In the following chapter, I explore the structure of the world of heroin and the general career of the addict then analyze how the woman fits into this world and addiction career. I begin by detailing the woman's entree into heroin and describe the process of inundation by the heroin world, work-activities and identities, difficulties in taking care of the business of mothering, and subsequent attempts out of heroin. Finally, I look closely at the ultimate narrowing of the woman's life options and the significance of this closure for her life as an addict and as a woman.

CHAPTER TWO

The Heroin World
and the Addict's Career

The nature of the heroin world has been described in detail in many ethnographies, among them: Agar's study of "ripping and running," Feldman's analysis of becoming an addict, Fiddle's study of the shooting gallery, Gould's study of connections, Hughes' study of copping networks, Preble's study of "taking care of business," and Sutter's analysis of the world of the "righteous dope fiend."[1] In these works, the addict is often described and portrayed, not as the down and out, passive degenerate of media publicity, but as an active, self-respecting, busy individual. Women are either omitted or seen as peripheral members of predominately male worlds, ornaments to lift the status and prestige of men, or money makers. No substantive description and analysis of women's experience in the heroin world, with the exception of James' work on prostitutes, has been done.[2]

It is unfair and inaccurate to assume that women experience the heroin world in the same ways that men do. Although heroin has been characterized as the great common denominator and there are structural conditions in the heroin world that exist for both sexes, women, in fact, confront different circumstances and social pressures. My research indicates that women addicts must relate to the world of heroin where the pace, norms, values, and patterns are shaped by men. Therefore, the heroin world as it is must first be understood and then analyzed to see how women fit into it. It is also necessary to look at how the career of the addict has been documented; it, like the heroin world, has focused on men. I look at what has been said about the male career in order to compare it with data about women.

The Heroin Lifestyle

Powerful structural conditions insure that many features of the heroin lifestyle are common to all addicts, men and women alike. The similarities in basic activities is mainly due to the illegality of heroin and fluctuating patterns of availability. Lindesmith depicts the general nature of the heroin lifestyle:

> The addict's time is broken up according to the demands of the habit, and days center on the times when he or she customarily "scores" with the "connection" or when he or she takes the shots. For the poorer addict, these "connections" are erratic and irregular due either to difficulties in raising the necessary money or in locating the elusive and suspicious peddler. In addition to these hazards, the addict must constantly be on the alert to avoid the police and the addicted "stool pigeons" who work for them. He or she must be ready to move at any moment, travel light, and if picked up be careful to have no incriminating evidence on his or her person. Addicts become exceedingly ingenious in all of these respects, so much so that even relatively unintelligent persons seem to have their dull wits sharpened by the need for dope. The drug user spends a good deal of his or her life inventing new devices and tricks and scheming and maneuvering to raise money to keep underworld connections and to evade detection.[3]

The addict lifestyle rotates around taking heroin for the purpose of alleviating withdrawal symptoms and/or getting high. Since heroin is an illegal substance, not purchasable either over the counter or through prescription, it must be obtained illegally. The cost is very high. Although the individual addict's habit varies greatly, a "bag" runs approximately $20, and depending on the quality of the heroin, an addict might use one to three bags per "fix." Depending on the length of addiction and the quality of heroin being used, an addict might "fix" from three to five times daily; thus, the addict's habit might range from $60 to $150 per day. The average job available to the addict pays nowhere near enough to cover food and shelter costs *and* heroin, so the vast majority of addicts resort to illegal occupations at some point and often throughout their heroin careers. These occupations are highly risky and often result in arrest and incarceration.

The addict's day often begins with withdrawal sickness: flulike symptoms, sometimes accompanied by vomiting or diarrhea. In order to alleviate these symptoms, the addict knows that s/he must use heroin. The symptoms become more intense with time; the longer the addict waits to inject the heroin, the worse withdrawal becomes. Therefore, if possible, the addict is out the door with the goal of buying heroin in order to feel well. There are, of course, personal variations to this scenario: If the addict is dealing heroin and it is in the house, it is possible to fix directly upon waking; or if the addict is organized, s/he may save some of the previous day's heroin for a wake-up fix. The addict may also have enough money from the previous day to buy heroin; otherwise, the addict awakens sick, has to go out and hustle enough money for a fix, then attempts to score (buy) heroin from the connection.

After the heroin has been purchased or taken out of the stash (supply), the somewhat time-consuming process of injecting or sniffing the drug begins. If the addict is sick, it is necessary to fix immediately upon purchasing the heroin. Thus, if home is not nearby, he may have to pay the connection (in the form of a portion of the heroin just bought) or a neighbor to use his/her home. The addict may also have to borrow or rent the paraphernalia ("works") necessary for injecting the heroin—usually a homemade syringe and hypodermic needle. When heroin is injected into the body, the user experiences a "rush," begins to "nod," and experiences the euphoric effects of the drug. The high lasts approximately four hours, then the scenario is played out once again: The addict begins to feel uncomfortable, then sick; s/he must go out and spend more money (this usually means more hustling) to buy the next fix. This is the addict's cycle—an existence almost literally from fix to fix—with the necessary heroin-related activities in between.

The Addiction Career

Much of the literature on addiction careers (also called life histories), as with other areas of addiction research, has taken a quantitive approach to data gathering—the survey. Often, this method is combined with the life-history interview.[4] From these studies and secondary analyses, a rather extensive body of literature on the addiction career has evolved.[5] Filling in the phenomenological holes are wholistic ethnographies[6] and those analyses of portions of the career.[7] Through these studies, which vary considerably depending on era, type of addict, geographic differences, and institutionalized versus street population, a limited male addiction career model has emerged. Drawing on previously cited research and theory on men the addiction career is traced in the following paragraphs.

The career is divided into five stages; they are succinctly: (1) an initial stage when people explore drug use lifestyles; (2) a "becoming" stage when regular visits into addict life are made as an apprentice;

(3) a "maintaining" phase when opiates are used regularly and the individual takes on an addict social identity and commitment; (4) an on again, off again stage when addicts slowly find drug use alternately functional and dysfunctional (this is usually accompanied by regular stays in jail and treatment centers); and (5) a conversion phase when the addict intends to become clean permanently.[8]

At the outset, the individual is socially amenable to the use of heroin. Educational progress has often (but not always) been stunted due to lack of encouragement, interest, or money, and consequently, occupational choices are limited to rather routine and mundane labor to which he makes little commitment. The future user often lives in a community where drugs in general and heroin in particular are omnipresent, thereby providing a readily available means for experimentation. Finally, if the casual use of a wide variety of drugs is sanctioned in the youthful segment of the community, the future user may stand to gain prestige and excitement from such experimentation or risk-taking. Even with these surroundings, most youths do not even experiment with heroin, and those who do experiment rarely become addicted; the *typical* heroin experience, therefore, ends without addiction.

After amenability to heroin (availability of drugs *and* openness to experimentation) and persistent use, the neophyte becomes addicted. This process occurs most often in spite of the individual's wish to remain in control and the sincere conviction that he has the power to do so. (Occasionally, the user wants to become addicted for social reasons—involvement, focus, purpose—and works very hard to do so. The purposeful user frequently becomes psychologically addicted before being physiologically habituated.) In a common scenario, the user experiences mild flulike symptoms and learns from an experienced user that these are withdrawal symptoms that can (only) be alleviated by heroin. At this point, the user either drops out of the addiction process or pursues the drug in order to get well. Having decided to stay "in," the user turned physiological as well as social addict finds that he is forced into a number of heroin-related activities that will both occupy the majority of his time and transform his identity.

The habituated individual begins to think of himself as an addict once immersed in the social world of addiction, a social world that was created when distribution, sales, and use went underground after the passage of the Harrison Act in 1914. An addict "argot" is used in this world as well as special techniques for buying and selling, for avoiding the police, and for the best use of the drug. This world is also characterized by forced exclusivity due to constant threat and risk. Through the use of special language and social interaction within the heroin world, the user begins to see other addicts as "significant others," thereby coming to see *himself* as an addict. The shift in identity can be temporary or long range, depending on the user's desire and success in ending or perpetuating the moral career in addiction.

If skillful, careful, lucky, and adept at taking care of business, an individual can maintain himself as an addict for years. Periodically, however, the heroin career is interrupted by abstinence in the form of involuntary incarceration (jail or prison) or treatment. While incarcerated, the addict kicks drugs (except in the rare instance in which heroin is accessible in prison, and even then, only a small habit can be maintained) and adapts to the jail or prison routine and ideology. Doing time in jail or prison socially redefines the addict as an outlaw: He has been arrested and convicted and, therefore, socially labeled. The addict is also forced to learn to function as a "right guy" in prison in order to survive, and this is tantamount to subscribing to the convict code and identifying with other outlaws.[9] Therefore, when the addict goes to jail or prison, his identity as a criminal is reinforced, which has implications for the direction he will take upon release.

An addict goes into treatment in order to clean up when he is "hot" with the police, having trouble getting drugs, or "burned-out" on the heroin life. Like getting *into* heroin, getting *out* through abstinence from drugs is a process: The addict may attempt abstinence and find that life without heroin is socially intolerable, the promise of the opiate-free life turns out to be hollow; or the ex-addict is disciplined enough to use heroin occasionally without becoming addicted. In any case, the recidivated addict has to be stronger with each attempt at abstinence, for he becomes less confident about the ability for long-term abstinence with each subsequent relapse or "fall."

The treatment mode itself seems less critical than the addict's own commitment to cleaning up and remaining abstinent. Moreover, the individual's addiction to the heroin life and lack of viable options outside are more important than the physiological habituation to heroin. If the addict is presented with viable social options outside the heroin life, he is more likely to end a career in drugs than the ex-addict who lacks such options. If he remains in the heroin life for a number of years, the aging addict often becomes tired and although having few other options, retires from heroin on his own initiative—often replacing it with a substitute drug.

The career of the addict involves socialization in a new occupation—drug use, beginning with initiation and followed by apprenticeship; it later involves full immersion in the world of heroin, including participation in illegal work (hustling), scoring, and administrating drugs. Inherent in these activities are arrest, incarceration, social labeling, and psychological identification with the addict world. The addict career, like other careers, involves building a social as well as psychological identity. Unlike the occupational or professional career, however, the addiction career is fraught with risk, danger, and unpredictability. Although in the beginning it is often these aspects that are attractive, ultimately the addict wants out. With time invested in the career, however, it becomes increasingly difficult to get out.

Where Are the Women?

How do women fare in the addict lifestyle and the heroin career? Where do they fit, and how do they deal with the exigencies of "the life?" In most of the preceding studies, women have been invisible at worst or peripheral at best. It has been assumed, therefore, that they either have to deal with the same conditions as men or they are not there at all; both assumptions are false. Women are very much there, and their lives as addicts are very different by virtue of the fact that they are women and have differing sets of concerns, options, and barriers. I begin the investigation by looking at how women get into the heroin world. The remainder of the book analyzes women's eventual inundation by addiction; their work; difficulties in taking care of business, especially children; attempts at getting out; and ultimately, the significance of their narrowing options both as addicts and straights.

CHAPTER THREE

Getting In

Life before Heroin

The beginning of any career (in legitimate as well as in deviant spheres) is preceded by a socialization process, which however long or short in duration, often lays the foundation for the ensuing career. I found that the aspect of women's lives (as well as of their male counterparts') that had the most direct bearing on their careers in heroin addiction was their membership in *social worlds* during their teenage and early adult years. The following excerpt from Lindesmith, Strauss, and Denzin defines the concept of social world as I use it:

> Social worlds [are] groupings of individuals bound together by networks of communication or universes of discourse. Whether the members are geographically proximate or not, they share symbolizations and hence, also share perspectives on "reality." It is significant that the term *social world* is often used in common parlance to refer to such abstract collectivities as the worlds of the theater, art, gold, skiing, stamp collecting, birdwatching, mountain climbing, and to occupational groupings like those of medicine and science. The concept, however, is equally applicable to almost any collectivity—including families, perhaps—if we emphasize communication and membership, for membership is not merely a matter of physical or official belonging but of shared symbolization, experiences, and interests.[1]

The social world that was of major import to the women prior to their experimentation with heroin is crucial to understanding their careers in addiction. For most of these women, the junior high school, high school, or neighborhood provided the social world to which they belonged. For some women, their social world overlapped with their school world, and for others, it was a retreat from an isolated school existence. Many women belonged to particular social worlds in order to find "action" or commonality; others drifted into worlds;

still others found themselves involved in social worlds because there were few other options for expression or belonging. For whatever reasons the women belonged, these worlds laid the foundation for careers in addiction.

Whether high school provided the setting for the social world or the impetus for dropping out and finding it elsewhere, the high school social system stands out as central in the formation of teenage social worlds. In a high school where there is a heterogeneous social class, there is a bipolar status system. As Irwin notes:

> The split in this system is related to the major class division of the student's parents—between the middle and working class. The pivots of the system are two leading figures—variously labeled soshes, elites, orgs, and bougies on the one side; and hoods, greasers, bads, vatos, esses, and pimps on the other. . . . The status hierarchy of the sosh end of the system is governed by a combination of characteristics—involvement in school activities, possession of prestige, winning personal characteristics, and material goods, proper grooming styles. . . . The other part of the system is analogous to working or lower-class culture. Participants value being "tough"—that is, willing to employ and confront physical force—or being "cool" or "sharp"—that is, imitating criminals, pimps, hustlers, dope fiends, and other recognized and admired "deviants."[2]

The working-class white women, Latinas, and some blacks in the sample population generally fell into the tough world, and their high schools and neighborhoods were dominated by hoods and "outlaws." The black women often dropped out of school early and, instead, identified with neighborhoods. The middle-class white women were often part of neither status system; they were not popular enough to make it with the soshes or with the toughs. These women often fled to the hippie scene for refuge from isolation in high school. In the following pages, I describe the three major social worlds to which the women belonged prior to their active involvement with heroin. I first examine the hippie trip; next, the outlaw world; and finally, the "fast life."

The Hippie Trip

Middle-class white women (19 percent of our population) often saw themselves primarily as hippies prior to their addiction to heroin. Many of these women were raised in rural or small suburban communities in northern California. They reported that their families were often strict, uncompromising, arbitrary, and lacked emotional commonality or sense of togetherness. The women rarely spoke of a bond with their families such as religion or joint activity; moreover, many of the women characterized themselves as social isolates. In the bipolar status system of their high school, they were neither part of the elite white crowd or the working-class toughs. Furthermore, the academic aspect of school was not attractive to them. Thus, school held little other than a sense of rejection, envy, and above all, boredom. These women felt that their lives were dull and that they had few ways to express themselves or importantly, to have fun.

The Haight-Ashbury hippie scene of the late 1960's looked extremely attractive to this type of girl.[3] All people, especially young women, were readily accepted. The hippie ethic had done away (at least ideologically) with the beauty criteria so pervasive in small-town high schools. Furthermore, the widespread use of drugs that was part of the hippie scene facilitated having the fun that was missed in high school.

Some women began to come regularly to San Francisco to attend functions such as concerts at the Fillmore Auditorium or Winterland; others left home completely in order to move to the Haight. Their exit or attempt to leave (parents often enlisted police to help bring them back) was an effort to expand options for activity and excitement. From a restrictive home life accompanied by little commitment to parents or parental values, the women came to the hippie scene and the freedom of San Francisco.

But by the time these women came to the Haight (the late 1960's and early 1970's), the scene had reached its demise.[4] The flower children had largely been replaced by "bikers" (motorcycle gangs) and hustlers. Often men from these groups would be most hospitable to girls coming to the Haight, and girls who had been rejected by the attractive and popular boys in their high school felt flattered by the attention of these older, experienced men. Frequently, white runaways became involved with bikers and hustlers, many of whom were selling drugs, and they, too, became involved in criminal pursuits. Sometimes the women were arrested and sent to youth prison; many were sent home, only to return again to the Haight. Through the runaway cycle, the women came into contact with the criminal justice system and convict identity long before they became involved with hard drugs.

Other women who became part of the hippie scene remained committed to orthodox hippie values and attempted to remain flower children even after the era had passed. They saw themselves primarily as poly-drug users rather than hardcore criminals. In sum, women who were involved in the hippie scene prior to using heroin tended to be the runaways or converts of the later 1960's and early 1970's who had left a small town and/or strict home and lonely social life for the excitement of drug use (marijuana, psychedelics, amphetamines, and barbiturates) and the ready acceptance that characterized the hippie scene.

The Outlaw World

The high school status system depends largely on the more general racial, ethnic, and social class constitution of the school. When the hoods or toughs outnumber the soshes, they tend to have power and prestige in the school.[5] Many women in this study were very much a part of their high school social scene as peripheral members of prestigious, tough, male gangs or more loosely structured groups. Although they referred to themselves and their male partners as outlaws, criminal activity was variable, and rather than necessarily indicating criminal pursuits, the term "outlaw" was equivalent to toughness, the willingness to engage in violence, and a variety of thefts.

An essential part of the outlaw world is the value placed on partying and having wild times. The use of several drugs, including marijuana, barbiturates, amphetamines, and less often, psychedelics and opiates is common among high school and young adult outlaws. School attendance is seen as less important than partying and truancy is common. School becomes a meeting place where drugs are purchased and taken, and the almost daily use of pills hampers attention if not attendance.

It is not uncommon for a woman who is involved in the outlaw world and using drugs daily for the sake of partying to have to drop out of school. Continual truancy and using drugs make it quite difficult for her to remain in school even if she is motivated to do so. In addition, finances often prohibit the woman from staying in school; she must work (generally at a menial job) or become involved in criminal activity such as boosting (shoplifting) on a full-time basis. Occasionally, a woman will opt to leave school (and home) in order to get married, have a baby, and become a certified adult.

Women constitute the "old lady" complement of the outlaw world. There is often violence among the women themselves, but they play a somewhat traditional role relative to the men's violent and criminal pursuits. Women often carry the drugs and shoplift, but when there is a real caper (burglary or robbery), they are left behind. Although they are becoming more involved in the criminal aspects of gang activities,[6] they are still lesser participants. The young women who become involved in criminal activity are usually arrested for petty crimes and sentenced to the youth authority. Here they become more committed outlaws and further enmeshed in the criminal world.

In sum, many women reported that they had had an exciting pre-heroin experience: They had been part of a cohesive and active social group—the outlaws—where there was much partying and drug use. The women who belonged to such groups and gangs were, by and large, working-class white women and Latinas. They were part of high school social worlds where multi-drug use was valued and get-ting "all fucked up" was a common goal. Membership in the social world of the outlaw, replete with toughness, "badness," and wild times often laid a solid foundation for future experimentation with heroin.

The Fast Life

Poverty, violence, and stunted aspirations are inherent in the black ghetto.[7] Since the value of school attendance is questioned and the student's financial resources are often needed, the drop out rate is considerably higher in ghetto than in nonghetto communities. As a consequence, the neighborhood, and more specifically the street, becomes the focus of the teenage and young adult social world.

Since work success based on involvement and commitment as well as monetary gain is, by and large, lacking for most ghetto dwellers, a substitute model has emerged;[8] for the young man, it is the "cat," as Finestone notes:

> . . . the cat as a social type is the personal counterpart of an
> expressive social movement. The context for such a movement
> must include the broader community, which, by its policies of
> social segregation and discrimination, has withheld from indi-
> viduals of the colored population the opportunity to achieve or
> to identify with status positions in the larger society. The social
> type of the cat is an expression of one possible type of adapta-
> tion to such blocking and frustration, in which a segment of
> the population turns in upon itself and attempts to develop
> within itself criteria for the achievement of social status and the
> rudiments of a satisfactory social life. Within his own isolated

social world, the cat attempts to give form and purpose to dispositions derived from but denied an outlet within the dominant social order.[9]

In the world of the cat, style, quiet manipulation, and kicks (drug use) are highly valued. Equally esteemed is the exploitation of women through prostitution.

Young girls are attracted to the fast life as a refuge from poverty and violence at home. Their families of origin are sometimes disrupted, crowded, and lack financial support; occasionally, the girls are propelled out of their homes by violence and sexual assault. They are attracted to high-status cats or pimps in the neighborhood and the costly material possessions that they can provide—cars, clothes, and drugs.

Some girls who experience poverty and violence at home become pregnant at an early age in order to leave home and/or establish themselves as adults. Thus, they drop out of school and attempt to take on the adult responsibilities of parenthood in their midteens. In either situation, the young girl in the ghetto world often drops out of high school before she finishes. For her, the high-prestige neighborhood social world is more significant than the high school social system. This neighborhood is composed of the pimp and prostitute world on the one hand and life in the projects on the other. In the neighborhood social world, a high premium is placed on getting down (using drugs and experiencing a high); drugs are also a reward for the hard work involved in hustling.

The young woman in the ghetto who becomes part of the fast life sometimes becomes involved with prostitution through relationships with older men (high-status pimps) whom she finds attractive and whose attentions are flattering. Having left school, her time is spent hustling and getting down. Soon she is wearing expensive clothes, driving a nice car, and often traveling. She has become part of one of the worlds in the ghetto that affords her respect and sustained excitement; it also provides entree into heroin use.

In sum, the fast life is one of the few attractive options open to the young woman in the ghetto. Although her relationship to men, particularly pimps or would-be pimps, is exploitative, it provides her with material possessions she lacks outside the life. Proximity to drugs is inherent in the ghetto world, and drug use is valued in those segments of the ghetto where societal values have been restructured to conform to the realities of poverty and blocked access.

Initially Reduced Options

The women in this survey population, particularly those who were black and Latina, came from relatively poor homes; their parents, by and large, worked at blue-collar and menial jobs. As a consequence, these women were not privy to the initial advantages of middle and upper middle-class women. Instead, the women were often subject to their parents' frustrations over too little money and too much work at jobs to which they attached little commitment or meaning. Most of these women grew up in homes where survival was the main task and all other aspects of life were considered almost frivolous; in addition, alcohol and drug use were commonplace. Consequently, earning money (through whatever means) at the earliest possible age was deemed more beneficial than finishing school.

The option to continue education was often eliminated when the young woman was encouraged to drop out of school in order to find a job and help support herself and the family. Sometimes the girl herself would initiate dropping out when it interfered with her social life and/or criminal activities. For whatever reason, many women did not finish high school (sometimes until they were in prison), thus functionally reducing their options for nonmenial work to which they might become committed.

The oppressive home life experienced by many of the women interviewed made them feel constricted and tied down. Occasionally, a woman married and/or became pregnant at an early age in order to leave her parents' home and establish her own household. With early motherhood and a stifled education, women's social and occupational options begin to funnel. With the job market shrinking in all sectors, occupational options are further reduced. Adler notes:

> . . . expanding technologies, shrinking frontiers, and cultural changes in industrialized nations have reduced the number of unskilled jobs while increasing the number of girls seeking employment. Never have so many young women had so much incentive to abandon traditional roles and so comparatively few opportunities within the system to find others.[10]

The initially reduced options of the women often had direct bearing on their membership in the social worlds discussed. The hippie attempted to create options by leaving a strict family and isolated home life. The outlaw dropped out of school in order to pursue the more lucrative monetary gains of criminal life as well as the excitement of the outlaw world. The woman entering the fast life did so in order to escape poverty and gain prestige in the community. Due to their initially reduced options resulting from poverty, lack of viable goals, work, and education, these women became enmeshed in social worlds that they felt could increase their options. It is within these social worlds, all replete with drug use, that they confronted still another option—experimentation with heroin.

Trying It Out

Personality vs. Social Process

A significant branch of research on causes of drug addiction has focused on preexistent motives as a rationale for experimentation with heroin (and other drugs). Several studies indicate that such motives as instant achievement, psychological support, imitation, thrill seeking, relaxation, recreation, and sense of well-being characterize the experimenter's frame of mind upon first using heroin.[11]

Others argue that initiation into drug use is a social process and should be analyzed in this light.[12] Blumer debunks the notion of preexistent motives specifically:

> It should be evident . . . that induction into juvenile drug use is a complex social process and not a simple matter of a youngster just going out and getting drugs to satisfy any of such presumed motives as curiosity, or the wish for excitement or self-destruction, or vengeance on society, or of "wishing to get away from it all," or of self-surrender to defeat. . . . One must view the recruitment of youngsters into drug use in the group context in which such recruitment actually goes on, and recognize that such recruitment is fundamentally a matter of being able to move into an already existing world and structure of drug use.[13]

Many researchers agree with Blumer that initial heroin use is social and that once heroin appears on the scene and the negative images have been debunked, an individual might try it out of curiosity.[14] Using heroin may be the "cool" thing to do in a social group, and it may represent rather bold and challenging play.[15] The literature on women's motivation for initial use of narcotics is sparse and focused on the psychiatric arena. In general, the woman heroin addict is regarded as sicker than her male counterpart, and accordingly, her motive for using narcotics is to escape reality, due to immaturity and incomplete psycho-sexual development. The woman addict has traditionally been seen as more passive than the man and thus, introduced to heroin either through medical complications or involvement with a male user. Consistent with the definition of women's entree into heroin as a seeking out of the drug, an addictive personality has been attributed to the woman addict. This personality trait has been given as the reason for the woman's initial and subsequent heroin use as well as for her failure to abstain.

Because my research was based on sociological assumptions of human activity, I searched from the outset for social patterns and processes that could explain and more sharply define the phenomenon under study. However, previous psychological research on women and heroin addiction loomed large overhead as the major research findings in the field. Thus, while looking for social process, I also considered psychiatric and psychological variables that might motivate an individual, particularly a woman, to use heroin. My data, admittedly sociological in focus, overwhelmingly indicated social roads into heroin addiction: the social worlds to which the women belonged, their relationship with a (male) partner, and often both.

I begin by looking at patterns of entree that characterize women's experience and within the discussion of these patterns, examine the social-psychological aspects of initial heroin use. I am dealing here specifically with women's perceptions of narcotics and addiction and the relevance of these perceptions to initial drug use. I then turn to the apprenticeship stage in the process of becoming an addict: the timing, drug use patterns, perceptions of addictive symptoms, and finally, the crucial factor—the joys of heroin.

Social Worlds

The Hippie Trip. For women who were part of the hippie trip, initial heroin use was an extension of an already vast amount of drug experimentation: They regularly used marijuana, LSD, and very often, amphetamines, and barbiturates. The context of this drug experimentation was social, usually in groups of three or four men and women.

Two major factors made those women who first used heroin via the hippie trip amenable to experimentation with narcotics. In the first place, the assumption that one might be deterred from using heroin by its addictive powers is questionable. The drug information disseminated in junior high schools and high schools during the late 1960's and early 1970's in an effort to curb rising rates of drug experimentation by teenagers may have, indeed, been counterproductive. The information was often erroneous—the insistence that, for instance, marijuana was addictive and LSD would cause mental illness and suicide. Heroin was labeled instantly addictive and the end point of involvement with other drugs. The popular image was the junkie undergoing withdrawal in a slum back alley. Many teenagers experimented with drugs, especially marijuana and LSD, and found that these drugs did not live up to the image portrayed in the drug information films and lectures; to the contrary, marijuana was rather benign and certainly not addictive. Having personally learned that the information received about marijuana was deceptive, many women reported believing that this information must be questioned with regard to *all* other substances. Thus discounting all establishment information opened the door to widespread experimentation with a large number of drugs, including heroin. Drug information shifted to the street, and individuals who were part of the hippie scene depended on each other for guidance in their drug use. In the street system, while heroin retained its position as a drug qualitatively different from other counterculture substances such as marijuana and "speed," it was no longer to be avoided a priori, since it had been given a worse reputation than warranted. One woman stated:

> Everything I learned in high school was bullshit. . . . I mean, they told me I'd get strung out on weed. . . . I didn't learn anything but lies in high school except maybe how to spell. I learned [about drugs] in the streets, from my friends. They used drugs and they knew what they were talking about.

Although there were a few women who claimed that they had no knowledge of heroin's addictive powers or that they discounted this information with other drug propaganda, most women did know that heroin was addictive. Two facets of heroin addiction were, however, unclear: an understanding of the *meaning* of addiction and the significance of addiction for the individual. Very few of the young white women involved in the hippie scene had ever known an addict firsthand; their basis of information about addiction came from such films as *Reefer Madness*, which they discounted as establishment bunk. Thus, the actual experience of addiction and the meaning of becoming addicted was unclear to these women. However, even if they had understood that heroin was addictive and that addiction was a state to be avoided, they had felt able to control their use of heroin in order to remain unaddicted. Because heroin was to be experimented with like other substances and a long-term "run" was not anticipated, most women felt that they could "chippy" or play around with heroin without becoming addicted. Not having been addicted before, they were unable to perceive symptoms of addiction; in fact, many chippied for long periods of time without knowing they were addicted until they experienced withdrawal symptoms. As one woman put it:

> They used to tell us that if you shot up one time, you were going to be hooked for life. It can only be true in a long-range sort of viewpoint. In other words, you are taking a first step. By shooting up, you are taking a first step towards a long-range downfall. It's not going to turn you into a dope addict. . . . maybe because so many people have the idea that it's long-range that they think they are the ones able to fool around with it. They think, "It's not going to affect me." They think they're the one person who can handle it. People should be set straight on this. You don't turn into a dope fiend instantly. . . . almost everybody I knew went through a long period of fooling around with it and other drugs. They were chippying. It's a gradual thing.

The very fact that heroin was introduced to the woman through her friends in the hippie scene almost automatically changed the definition of the situation. Heroin probably did not have all the characteristics predicted by sources outside the scene; at any rate, it was not to be an exclusively ghetto drug. Heroin was, in fact, being passed around with those other familiar substances in the company of one's close companions, which transformed it from an untouchable drug into one of many to be tried and used as part of the drug culture of the hippie scene in the late 1960's and early 1970's. One woman said:

> He'd been a medic in Vietnam and that kind of made it safe to me. He'd learned venipuncture in the Army. It was as though he was a doctor. He was white, came from a Jewish family (my background's Jewish), and was well-educated. It wasn't a real sleazy, lower-class scene.

Outlaws. As noted earlier, women from working and lower-class neighborhoods as well as Latinas often went to high schools where the toughs or outlaws were powerful, respected, and had prestige. Extensive drug use was part of the high school and neighborhood outlaw world; in fact, many women described their high schools as rampant with drugs. A wide variety of substances could be purchased on the campus, including heroin. Most important, if the social group was "into" a certain drug, the entire group would be expected to try it. Heroin would often pass through a group, and nearly everyone would experiment with it as in the hippie trip; heroin was seen as simply part of an array of drugs that was currently on the scene and hence to be tried.

The Fast Life. The use of narcotics and involvement in criminal activity are largely overlapping areas. While building an expensive heroin habit often necessitates criminal activity for its support, as will be discussed later, many individuals are already involved in the criminal world *prior* to using narcotics. In the population, several women (largely older whites, blacks, and Latinas) had been involved in criminal pursuits, generally prostitution, before using heroin; they were already in the life when they were initiated to heroin and were generally initiated by close friends—both male and female—who were already addicted. I do not wish to suggest that ghettos are filled with heroin and residents become addicted through osmosis. The majority of the people in such communities are not addicted and have never even tried heroin. My point is that for ghetto women there is often a proximity to narcotics as there is a proximity to the criminal activity generated by poverty and discrimination; therefore, the presence of heroin in the lives of women who are already living in a scene containing at least moderately widespread heroin use is not in question. A woman who is already in the (drug/fast) life is surrounded by heroin from the time she enters the scene;[16] she is likely to be introduced to heroin use at a party where someone brings it out for others to share. Another common mode of initiation is by the woman's spouse, friend, or date.

Individual Partners

In many earlier studies of addiction, it has been argued that women are generally initiated into heroin use through a man—a lover, spouse, boyfriend, "old man";[17] the image presented is that of a rather passive woman "turned on" to illicit activities by her man. My data indicate that this picture is far from accurate—particularly for women in the sample who are under 25 and typically, were members of the social worlds previously described.

Those women who *were* introduced to heroin exclusively by their man tended to be somewhat older than women introduced to heroin in other ways; the former had first used heroin prior to 1970 and had done little group experimentation with girlfriends or in large social groups. Women introduced to heroin by a spouse tended to have done so prior to the impact of the women's movement (they could not be considered "liberated") and without involvement in the hippie scene or criminal activities. They were somewhat traditional women—maybe housewives and mothers—in a marital or semi-marital relationship with an addicted man, yet none were passive. I learned of no incident where a woman was forced to try heroin. Instead, it was usually *she* who instigated the introduction.

There are three common motives for a woman living with an addict to get into heroin: dealing, wanting to share a mood, or wanting a share of the "money" (drugs become money). If a man is dealing heroin, it is likely to be plentiful in the house; the woman is also very likely to be involved in cutting and bagging the drug and making sales contacts. The availability of heroin makes it tempting to try at least once. Another common reason for a woman to encourage her spouse to introduce her to heroin is his preoccupation with the "high" and hustle that characterize addiction. Addicts tend to have little time for other kinds of activities, so the woman married to or living with an addict is often very lonely—psychologically if not physically. She may feel that she is not part of her man's "trip" and want to get down with him—to understand what he is experiencing; therefore, she may encourage him to let her use some of his heroin so they can get down together. Even a woman who is not particularly interested in using heroin herself may begin to resent the financial drain on her family due to the great expenditures for heroin. She may decide that if all the money coming in is spent on heroin, she is entitled to reap whatever benefits exist. In all these instances—being the dealer's old lady, curiosity about the drug, wanting to share the experience, or wanting part of the goods for which the money is spent—the woman is introduced to heroin by her spouse who is already addicted, but it is *she* who initiates the encounter. Indeed, very few men want their wives or women to become addicted: It is a worse financial drain and much more difficult to maintain any semblance of routine family life with *two* addicts in a family. It is very often the case, therefore, that the woman coaxes the man to *let* her use some of the heroin, rather than the popularly depicted scenario where a man coerces a resisting woman to use heroin.

Expanding Options

Initial experimentation with heroin may provide a woman with several new life options. A very young girl may want to affiliate herself with addicts in order to boost her status in the community. She may think that all the cool people are addicts, so that is what she also wants to be. One woman pointed out:

> When I was 17, my girlfriend brought this guy over, real nice looking guy—the first fine looking dude I'd ever seen in my life. He was my idol. So I did it [heroin] and it was just utopia. I was sitting up in this chick's room. She had silk sheets on the bed—totally organic—and it just seemed pure and right, organic heroin and organic drugs and these two beautiful people.

If addicts appear to be successful and addiction rewarding, a woman might intentionally become an addict. To a relatively poor young girl with few options, the fast life and heroin use may seem quite attractive. Involvement in this scene may be her only opportunity to wear expensive clothes and drive an expensive car; she may find the members of this world attractive and friendly, and experimenting with heroin may increase the opportunity of having an enduring love relationship. The prospect of entering the heroin world may also provide the focus and commitment lacking in other social worlds and aspects of the woman's life. In short, initial heroin use may be part of a world that a young woman enters willingly and purposefully because it is more attractive, rewarding, and accessible than any other open to her. At this point in the woman's career, her options are broadest; the mouth of the funnel that is illustrative of her career is at its widest. It is after the woman becomes addicted that her life options begin to narrow.

Getting Hooked

> You don't wake up one morning and decide to be a drug addict. It takes at least three months' shooting twice a day to get any habit at all. . . . You become a narcotics addict because you do not have strong motivations in any other direction. Junk wins by default. I tried it as a matter of curiosity. I drifted along taking shots when I could score. I ended up hooked. . . . You don't decide to be an addict. One morning you wake up sick and you're an addict.[18]

It is entirely possible for an individual to be introduced to heroin without ever becoming addicted, which is the case with the majority of people—both men and women—who ever try it. Becoming addicted is a process that, for the beginning user (ex-addicts who have been clean for a long period of time become readdicted much faster than the novice), is rather slow. It takes *time* to become an addict, and it is the lapse of time between initial use and recognition of addiction that is puzzling to onlookers, particularly to those who have never experienced heroin addiction. The question most often posed is, "Knowing that heroin is addictive, why would the beginner continue to use the drug?" I have attempted to answer this question in a systematic and scientific fashion to little avail. As a phenomenologist, I first went to the women and asked them, "Why did you continue to use heroin knowing its addictive powers?" Save for the few women who deliberately wanted to become addicts for reasons already discussed, the majority claimed they did not realize that they were becoming hooked. I found that the most useful approach was to look at the question critically, so I turned back to the original tenet of the study: Heroin addiction was to be studied, *not* as a problem per se, but as a phenomenon; not from a correctional perspective, but with appreciation.[19] I constantly looked for the positive aspects of being an addict, specifically a woman addict. It was necessary to purge myself of middle-class, never-have-been-addicted assumptions about addiction and go from there. As will become apparent later, purging my own biases about being addicted was a difficult endeavor. The women *themselves* refused to let me view addiction positively; getting high was positive but not being addicted. The problem with heroin— and this is a critical point—is that in order to experience it to the fullest, the novice has to use the drug *continually* over an extended period of time. It is the attempt to derive the fullest euphoria from the drug that helps to explain the process of becoming addicted; the intense excitement of experiencing a new drug, a new high, also draws people into prolonged and persistent heroin use. In the following paragraphs, I examine three variables that are crucial to the process of becoming an addict, for both women and men: timing of drug use, drug use methodology, and perception of euphoric/addictive symptoms.

Timing

After an individual is introduced to heroin, s/he must use it over and over again before becoming addicted. The timing of subsequent heroin use has direct bearing on whether and when the individual will become addicted. I found two different basic timing patterns: using intermittently (chippying) and persistantly. Most women interviewed in this study had chippied with heroin before using it on a daily basis over a prolonged period of time. A very common mode involved trying heroin at one point and then not using it again until several months later. A woman might dabble in heroin in this fashion for months or years without becoming addicted. Several researchers have found that the most common type of male heroin user is the experimenter rather than the addict,[20] which is consistent with my findings about women.

A woman may purposely control her use of heroin in order *not* to become addicted. In this situation, she will use heroin one day and then not use again, for instance, for two days. She usually has a relatively stable lifestyle at this point, but a problem in her life—loss of job, family difficulties—can provide the rationale for giving up and using daily until she is addicted. One woman described her experience:

> I knew there was something lacking in my life at that time. I needed something more. I wanted to go out, do things. I mean, I loved my baby. I didn't mind taking care of him. But other than that, I had nothing. And that's when I started snorting [heroin] and replacing all the things I felt I was missing with being loaded all the time.

A key variable in chippying versus daily use is availability: If heroin is not available after the initial experience, the initiate cannot use again until it is available. Many women began daily use immediately because heroin was readily available—they were living with a dealer. In many of these cases, the women skipped the chippying period altogether and began daily use at the outset.

It is quite common for an individual to try heroin and not experience a high; vomiting is more usual on first use than the euphoria which is supposed to characterize heroin. If a woman has access to heroin over a prolonged period of time, she may keep on using heroin until she finally gets over the vomiting and is able to experience the euphoria that she perceives her friends are experiencing. One woman said:

In the beginning, I was into spacing it, but I wanted to see what was so great. I thought I hadn't done enough or I'd done too much; maybe it was the circumstances, maybe my body wasn't used to it. You have to know what to look for, you can't really get high unless you've experienced it and know what to focus on.

Belief in one's own immunity characterizes most men's attitudes about becoming addicted after persistent heroin use. As Duster notes:

The individual user never believes he himself will become addicted. Perhaps we see here the same mechanism that allows a soldier on a battlefield to surge forward and continue fighting while he sees soldiers around him dying from wounds. One can be firmly set in the belief that the self is inviolable, unique, and not subject to suffering, accident, or death. It is unlikely that traditional ground wars could be fought unless men believed that they personally would not die on the battlefield.[21]

The majority of the women interviewed did not set out to become addicted; they, too, believed that they would not become addicted. It is this sense of immunity to addiction, of the power to control usage, that opens the door to prolonged experimentation. It is ironic that this sense of immunity precedes addiction, because it is only prior to addiction that one is immune to the heroin "yen." One addicted woman reflected:

I think that like all people that first get into it, you think that you will never be a victim of this. "I can handle it." I don't know any heroin user when they start out that doesn't feel this. There is no way that you can tell anybody differently. I had the same attitude, the same attitude that I would be different. I would be able to handle it; it would never dominate me.

In order to experience heroin's euphoria to the fullest, however, one must be a seasoned user, and by the time one becomes seasoned, a habit, however mild, has been started.

It has been argued in prior comparative studies of men and women addicts that women become addicted *faster* than men;[22] however, women's differential access routes into heroin have direct bearing on the speed with which they become addicted. They tend to have drugs provided for them for a longer period of time than is characteristic of men's initial drug use. In addition, a woman who lives with a dealer or an addicted man has access to heroin on a daily basis for very long stretches of time, so she can, therefore, use heroin daily until she builds up a habit.

Drugs have a cyclic quality: At a given time, certain drugs will become plentiful in a community. I have learned, for example, that from 1968 to 1975 heroin was plentiful in San Francisco and the quality was high. Over the past three years, however, the quality has declined and the price has been inflated. The majority of women in the sample had become addicted to heroin during the years when it was plentiful and of high quality; many, in fact, spoke of their initial and subsequent experiences as exciting times when heroin was tried by entire social groups. For some women, this stage was characterized as their honeymoon with heroin—a time when they partied and used heroin every day; it was exciting, a new experience, something to look forward to. As one woman noted:

> So, I let this girl shoot me up. Then it started to be this everyday thing where I would do it [heroin] before work, and mostly after work, I would go over to their house and they would do me up. I would buy some and they'd do me up. My old man was suspecting this all along. He was still yelling about it. In fact, on the times that he got out of me that I did do some, he'd mark it down on the calendar. He'd go, "you don't do anymore now for a month, you know." He really wanted me to stop because he knew how bad it was. I couldn't understand how it could be that bad. I didn't feel any kind of a physical thing for it. But then it started getting so I was at work, and I was having a real shitful day. Like everything at work was bad, and I'd be thinking to myself, "Oh, as soon as I get out of here, I'm going over to so and so's house and I'm going to do some dope. I'll forget all about this crap." I made it a thing never to do any during the day or on the job, but every night I'd be going over to this guy's house and doing it. And I'd feel real good right away just thinking I would get high, so I noted I was getting a mental addiction; not a physical thing, but a mental thing.

During a time and social setting in which drug use was commonplace, heroin provided a high that was superior in quality to marijuana, amphetamines, barbiturates, and certainly LSD in terms of euphoric effect. Additionally, heroin differentiated the user from others in the drug world. In short, for women who were part of social groups that became involved with heroin while it was plentiful and of high quality, daily use was part of the honeymoon these women were on—the beginning and most intense phase of what would be their love/hate affair with heroin.

Drug Use Methodology

Drug use methodology is crucial to becoming addicted. Substances can be taken orally, smoked, sniffed, and injected; the *manner* in which heroin is taken has implications for recognizing addiction. Using a needle has great symbolic import in all drug cultures, as it is seen as the divider between using "hard" and "soft" drugs. The soft drug user takes drugs in any way *except* by injection; the hard drug user injects or tries to inject nearly any substance that s/he is using. Injection is seen as neater and more economical, since one wastes much less of the drug than by sniffing or "snorting." Additionally and more importantly, one experiences a decided rush from injection as opposed to the relatively slow effect time with other methods.

The pattern of entree into heroin use is often consistent with a particular methodology of drug use. Women who entered heroin use through the hippie scene very often used heroin in the same way that they had used cocaine—snorting. Due to methodology of intake, heroin, regardless of its known addictive qualities, remained for these women in a category with other softer, counterculture substances such as marijuana and LSD.

Methodology of drug use is important in the career of the addict. The woman who has a history of using drugs only by ingestion makes a symbolic break when she first "shoots up"; Alksne also found this to be the case with men.[23] The user then begins to think of herself as part of a qualitatively different social world—the world of the addict. Using a needle is an important symbolic break between hard and soft drugs, between the world of counterculture drug users and the junkie.[24] When a woman "fixes," she symbolically enters the world of narcotics. Several women noted that they had resisted using the needle for the expressed purpose of remaining *out* of the world of narcotics; they were also among those who believed that if they only snorted heroin and did not use a needle, they were immune to addiction. The longer the woman continued snorting, the longer she could put off having to adjust her self-concept to that of a hard drug user and eventually an addict. When the needle was first used to inject heroin, many women felt that a turning point had been reached in their lives; they felt vulnerable and open to addiction. A decided lack of control had come over their lives.

Women who began to use heroin after having been involved in the fast life had often used a needle to inject other substances, particularly amphetamines and methedrine (speed); for them, using the needle was casual, even sensible. Many were, in fact, substituting heroin for speed in order to "come down" from an intense dependence on amphetamines.

An important aspect of injecting heroin is the mode of injection. Most inexperienced users are shot up by someone else in the beginning; for women in particular, this pattern is often prolonged.[25] It is paradoxical that women who had independently initiated their use of heroin would subsequently become dependent on a man to inject the drug. My data indicate that this pattern has symbolic import: The dependency of the woman's addiction makes it somewhat less an addiction than if she were shooting up herself. One woman said:

> He didn't want me to start using, but I wanted to try it—and then, with time, I got hooked. But I made sure that he shot me up. I mean, I said at the time that he was better at it than me, but the real feeling I had was that if I couldn't even fix myself, I must not be a real junkie.

Many women who have consistently been fixed by others feel it is an important step in their careers when they first fix themselves. Their heroin use is redefined as a habit—something they have to attend to themselves, immediately; they can no longer wait for someone else to help them "get off." This can be a frightening realization. Women often believe that they have replaced one kind of domination with another—male domination with domination by a drug whose insistence they cannot control.

Perceiving the Symptoms

Addiction is a state of mind as well as a physiological condition. The experienced addict who is clean and begins to use heroin again knows the symptoms of addiction well and begins to experience them in a very short time.[26] In fact, some ex-addicts experience symptoms of addiction even when they have been clean for long periods of time. *Thinking* about heroin can produce symptoms of addiction.

For the novice, the symptoms of withdrawal are the indicators of addiction.[27] Many of the women interviewed claimed that they did not know they were addicted, sometimes for a very long period of time (months), until one day they could not get drugs, could not fix, and began to experience flulike symptoms. In most cases, the woman complained about these symptoms to a friend (an experienced user) who then informed her that what she was feeling was withdrawal—that she was addicted. Denial and surprise are two common responses to this news. The woman knows that she must take more heroin, then faster than with any medical remedy, her symptoms will be gone, almost magically; not only will her symptoms disappear, she will also feel psychologically high. Ultimately, attempts are made to "score" drugs in order to fix and get well. And so begins the scenario: waking up feeling sick, knowing that in order to get well she must get fixed, and going out with that purpose in mind—day in and day out. As this woman noted:

> I remember not using it for a day or so, I was working at the time. I thought at first I was coming down with a cold. My nose was running, I felt cold with the shivers and uncomfortable all over. I really didn't know very many heroin users at that time, so I wasn't really sure of just what the symptoms were. Somebody told me, "Well, you've got a jones." Well, of course, upon using again a few hours after that, my symptoms were alleviated. And the symptoms were fairly light because even though I'd been using daily, it had only been for a couple of months and a really small amount, so the symptoms were light. But, to me, it was an inescapable fact at that moment. That was what it was, you know; it was a physical addiction.

Although the vast majority of women did not realize they were addicted until experiencing withdrawal and being told by *someone else*, it seems that when the heroin user is able to experience heroin's euphoria to the fullest and without nausea (about three weeks), s/he is *already* (albeit slightly) addicted. Many women noted that they had to persist in using heroin before they could get down. This persistence results in simultaneous euphoria and addiction.

It is possible to have one (euphoria) without the other (addiction) through chippying, as is fairly common in controlled users only after having *already* been addicted at some point.[28] Past experience makes it possible to anticipate and immediately recognize heroin's euphoria and thereby get down without the persistent use that is necessary for the novice.

Being sick is the first sign of addiction for the novice, and this state has great importance, for it is both an indication of possessing a habit and a signal or warning of what is to come. Being sick is the initial dues the addict will pay for her career in drugs, and it is this sickness that will motivate her activities while she remains addicted. Being sick is the other side of the coin, but as long as she can remedy this sickness, she sees it as a mild price to pay for the high experienced on heroin.

The degree of sickness or withdrawal symptoms is a very important variable for the addict. The more heroin the addict has used, the more intense the withdrawal symptoms will be: The bigger the habit, the worse the withdrawal. The novice addict generally does not build up a big enough heroin habit to undergo intense withdrawal symptoms; instead, she experiences a mild cold—runny nose, watery eyes, sometimes diarrhea. The mildness of the sickness accounts for the surprise that these are indeed symptoms of a heroin habit, that she is hooked, and the subsequent calmness at the news. Withdrawal in the beginning is neither very intense nor painful; it is just being sick, and as one gets over a cold, one can get over this. For the novice, the anticipation of possibly getting sick and the subsequent reality of it are not sufficient deterrents. The implications of the act of using heroin persistently only become apparent at a more distant point in the addict's career. The novice finds the joys of heroin much greater than the small dues paid in the initial stages of use. As one woman reflected:

> And one morning, I woke up and I realized that I didn't feel good, and if we would have been smart, we would have stopped it right there. But not many of us are smart, 'cause we just go out and get that little fix, and all our aches and pains are gone. You know, you are not thinking that in five or six hours you are going to feel kind of bad again and you are going to want another fix, and we were just off and running. Eventually, we had to start paying for it, and there goes my house, my cars, my jewelry.

The Joys of Heroin

Many analyses of heroin addiction, particularly those dealing with the becoming stages, fall short in two ways. In the first place, a crucial element of the process is omitted when it is analyzed by a researcher who has never experienced a heroin high or been addicted—a description of that aspect of addiction that is, in fact, the *key* to becoming addicted: the *high*. Second, many researchers, by and large unfamiliar experientially with heroin, simply assume that they understand the nature and quality of the euphoria and go on from there. As an individual who has neither experienced a euphoria from heroin nor heroin addiction, I found the analysis of becoming an addict quite difficult, even armed with extensive phenomenological data. Fortunately, the women interviewed enjoyed elaborating on what I came to call the "joys of heroin," so I can proceed, admitting what I consider a handicap. I identified two aspects of the joys of heroin: social and psychological/physiological or as I will call them, "the life" and "the high."

The Life

As noted in my discussion of the timing in heroin use, the social aspects of heroin are important in becoming an addict. Heroin often appears in social groups, and there is an excitement among group members about its appearance. The beginning user also enters the already established social world of heroin. She learns about the nature of this social world at a point in her own life when she is usually young and relatively healthy. The world of heroin can look very inviting at this stage, as one of the women related:

> Both these chicks at the massage parlor had already been strung out, and I really loved them chicks. . . . like I thought they were so beautiful. I looked up to them. They couldn't do no wrong by me. Everything they did was right to me, so I just went ahead and went right along with them.

The social world of heroin (and concomitant crime, I should add), which I will refer to as the life, is a world of fast-moving excitement, prestige, money, and material possessions. The heroin life is also very busy: Many women noted that they became busier than they had even been when they began to use heroin on a daily basis. There is a lot to learn at first: how to find a "connection" from whom to buy drugs; how to get enough money to buy drugs; how to cop drugs inconspicuously; how to administer drugs. All of this is taught by an experienced user, either male or female, whose prowess is admired. Many women characterized this learning stage as exciting. It also made them feel that they had entered a "demiworld" full of secrets and codes, that with this new membership, they were a peg above mundane people living dull lives. The women often felt that they were cleverly pulling the wool over the eyes of those around them, and they found this exciting. Another woman said:

> Sometimes it's cool, it's real cool. My home town ain't that big. It's a university town and half the population is kids, and they're all looking up to their rock star idols. Jimi Hendrix, walking down the street all fucked up [on heroin], compared to all these college kids who are thinking they're so bad, and they don't know jack shit.
>
> I knew I wanted to get addicted. Everyone who goes into it knows that they must want to get addicted. In the beginning when I was snorting it, I knew I didn't want to start hitting it up because I'd get addicted. So, I justified that as long as I was snorting, I didn't care how much I used because I didn't believe you could really get that bad off if you stayed away from needles. Ever since the fifth or sixth grade you hear the worst thing, the most far out thing is heroin, so I felt, "Oh, I'm finally here, far out! I've gone all the way away—I'm totally away from my father and society, free from all that shit now."

Often women characterized their entree into the life as a time of celebration when they partied every day and had a lot of fun. Their days became filled with the new activities of hustling to get money, then scoring, and finally, the event that they had looked forward to—fixing and getting down. Many women's lives became more intense, meaningful, and fulfilling than they had ever been. As one woman put it:

> It's very time consuming. . . . you don't have a chance to get into other things. Even if you're selling drugs and making it [money] that way, you still have to take lots of time to sell. It's very busy. That's why I think a lot of people get drawn into it and stay into it, because it does occupy your time. You don't have time for anything else; it saves you from being bored.

Women who were associated with dealers during the beginning stages of their addiction, had access to more money than they had ever seen. Often for the first time, they had nice clothes, a car, and a nice place to live because they were making more money than before. As this woman noted:

> I had a Cadillac. He had bought me a Cadillac. I was dressing right, and we were driving around all the time, goin' out to

nice clubs, and things like that. We traveled a lot. I've been to
New York. I've seen New Orleans. I've been back to Chicago.
That kind of made me up in the life—up with the *big time*
people. We used to go out to the Players Ball. All the big time
people go out there and sell drugs and everything. I kind of
liked that.

In sum, during the beginning stages of heroin addiction, for both
men and women, one aspect of the joys of heroin is the social world
of addiction—the life. This life, characterized by many women as exciting, fun, a peg above the mundane, filled with money, material
goods, activity, and something to look forward to every day, is especially attractive to a poor woman who is either jobless or bored
with her work and not reaping many of the advantages that this society has to offer.

The High

In my head, I equate it with sex because you don't really feel
the drive or the need until you get into it, and then it becomes
very compulsive and very sensual—a release. You take risks,
give up a lot of things for it. It becomes very vital. After I got
into it, I had hepatitis. . . . and I've gone through these really
heavy, crazy trips, and I say, "I should learn from this." But it's
like trying to be celibate if you've gotten high on sex. It becomes part of your life, my life, and I realize that I can't say I'm
never going to do it again. At first, when I would kick, I would
say that I was never going to do it again. If I say that, I'll try
not to do it for a long time, but I know if I'm feeling heavy
emotional pain or physical pain, that's where I'm going to turn
to. It's like a security base, and I know it's there so I can avoid
feeling a lot of pain. Something that feels so good, it's hard to
say I'm going to deny myself. On days when I don't use it, I
think about it every day, I dream about it. It's part of who I am.

The euphoric effects of heroin are both physiological and psychological. When fixing heroin, one first feels the rush—that point when
the heroin enters the bloodstream, which is almost immediately, and
produces an initial jolting sensation, followed by a taste in the back of
the mouth, and a relaxing of the entire body. One feels a calm over
the body—the sensation that everything is moving in slow motion.
Some women equate the heroin rush to a sexual sensation. Many
women claimed that they felt energetic on heroin—that they were

motivated to do housework. Heroin relieves bodily symptoms of disease such as arthritis and bronchitis; it is also powerful enough to cause amenorrhea. One woman said:

> For myself, the biggest thing was that it gave to me a feeling of physical well-being. It's hard to say how much of a feeling of mental well-being, although that certainly must have been there. All my adult life, I've been very sensitive to cold for instance. It was like even on the coldest night you felt a sense of warmth. It gave me a lot of energy, but it wasn't the same nervous energy that you had from speed. You could do your housework without feeling tired or anything. There was just a sense of physical well-being that is a notch above what most people feel on the natch.

The physiological effects of heroin seem to have a direct bearing on the user's psychological perspective. Many women discussed the way in which the relief from bodily tension, which results from the relaxing effect of heroin, caused relief from the tension produced by interacting with others. As one woman noted:

> It was easier to get loaded than to fight with my old man. . . . he would encourage me to get high just so I'd stop being a bitch.

Heroin creates a feeling of generalized well-being—one hasn't a care in the world, there are no responsibilities, and nothing really matters. It is an extremely peaceful feeling, one in which everything is somehow magically okay; one woman related:

> It's just a good feeling. At that particular time, shit, you don't have a problem in the world. Nothin'. I heard a doctor say right here in this jail that heroin preserves people. You are not sick. You don't feel pain. Fuck the rent, fuck the food, fuck the phone, fuck the kids, fuck how you look. Really, it's just an "aw, fuck it" attitude. At the time you are loaded, nothing bothers you.

Heroin is truly the king, better in quality of high—both physiologically and psychologically—than other commonly used substances such as alcohol, marijuana, barbiturates, amphetamines, psychedelics.[29] The user experiences an overwhelming sense of well-being without the sloppiness of drunkenness, the speed of amphetamines, the drowsiness of barbiturates, or the disorientation of psychedelics. As this woman said:

The first time I did it, I threw up, but I felt great. The body sensation is like you are laid back. It's the opposite of acid; acid intensifies everything. This blurs everything—nothing bothers you. You're in nirvana. You lay back, you nod, you dream. I've watched people OD in front of me, and it's as though you're moving in slow motion. It's no big deal. You see this person turning blue, then you think, "Okay, I've got to help this person. I've got to give them mouth to mouth." But it's [heroin] got you so calm yourself that you know normally you'd probably freak out. It's just real nice. I know it hurts me and I know it's an escape. I admit that to myself. I still go back to it.

And another woman pointed out:

You could go into a crowd and ask somebody a question and not be embarrassed. You could sit in a restaurant and nod in your soup and that's okay too.

Irwin also discusses the phenomenon of not caring as one of the attractions of the dope fiend lifestyle:

Being removed from all care is a category of the drug life that has not received enough attention, despite the fact that it is very important. The best way to convey the meanings related to not caring is in stories told by addicts themselves. The following is one such story from the many I have heard on this subject:
    A lot of times I've gone on the nod in restaurants. One time, I ordered some food because I thought I was hungry. But when the chick brought me the food, I was going on the nod. Pretty soon my head started sinking down on the counter and my face ended up in the food. After awhile, I guess, I came back out of the nod and looked around. A lot of people were looking at me. There I was with food all over my face. Everyone was embarrassed, but not me. I just wiped off the food with my napkin and sat there. I didn't give a fuck. When you're loaded that shit just doesn't bother you.[30]

Conclusion

The reasons for getting into heroin addiction have their bases in women's social circumstances and the social worlds to which they belong. It is largely due to social class and economic situation that women addicts were part of the outlaw and ghetto (fast life) worlds. Middle-class isolates drifted into the hippie world seeking refuge from more traditional high school worlds where they could not succeed. Membership in each of these worlds made commitment to school difficult; furthermore, using drugs and partying were valued. And since little value was placed on education, many women dropped out of school, thereby reducing their occupational options. Hence, women's lives before heroin involved membership in social worlds where they were confronted with drugs, including heroin, in an amenable setting that presented few competing options.

Women often try heroin for the first time within these social worlds, and they are often introduced to the drug by a male partner within that world, but this is highly variable. The amenability to experimentation with heroin is a result of many factors, including a disregard for antiheroin propaganda; the value placed on drug use within a given social world; wanting to share with a lover, and the desire to expand one's options for experience, belonging, money, and other material goods.

A woman can and often does chippy with heroin for long periods of time. However, if heroin is on the scene in large quantities, she may use it persistently over a period of time. Since many women are unable to experience the euphoria for which heroin is renowned during the first few times, they persist until they think they have achieved the heroin high. Although most women feel they are immune to addiction, they get caught or hooked if they persist in using heroin.

Drug use methodology is important in addiction. The user often believes that if heroin is taken in any way other than injection, it is less likely that she will become addicted; many women attempt to stay away from needles for this reason. This assumption is, in fact, false, and the women do become addicted. Beginning needle use is regarded as a major transition. Once a woman begins to fix heroin, she sees herself as qualitatively different than the counterculture or soft drug user. She often ceases to even attempt to retain the softer identity and begins to think of herself as a junkie, a full-fledged addict, as many women put it.

Withdrawal symptoms are usually the woman's first indication that she is addicted. She experiences flulike symptoms, reports them to a knowledgeable friend, and learns that she has a habit; she also learns that this form of sickness can be cured instantly with heroin.

And so begins the process of further addiction. The woman's career as an active heroin addict has officially begun.

It is not a mournful situation at this point, for in the beginning the woman is in the honeymoon stage of her marriage to heroin. She experiences the pure joys of heroin: the life, with all its excitement, activity, money, partying. She feels she is part of a demiworld that is a cut above the mundane. Finally, she experiences the high, a smoothing out of an otherwise rough world, the elimination of all problems and worries in an inward focus that is sublime and ecstatic in nature.

The literature and my data indicate that becoming addicted—both socially and physiologically—is experienced very similarly by men and women. The differences become more marked later in the career when the toll of the heroin life affects women more severely and their roles as mothers and women impede their ability to "keep it together" as an addict.

CHAPTER FOUR

Risk, Chaos, and Inundation

The beginning addict, as noted earlier, is provided a ready focus and commitment when she becomes addicted to heroin. Part of the willingness, sometimes eagerness, to become addicted lies in a key aspect of the heroin world—its riskiness: The daily excitement of getting away with illegal heroin use can make the life attractive. The risk that using heroin involves has, however, several other consequences. Due to the constant threat of detection and arrest, heroin users are forced to be selective in their associations. Care must be taken to avoid doing business with plain-clothes policemen/women and other potentially threatening figures. The risk works in two ways. While addicts fear exposure to the conventional world and the possibility of subsequent arrest and incarceration, nonaddicts often fear exploitation and theft *by* addicts. Consequently, addicts and nonaddicts tend to stay away from each other, so for the addict, an insulated social world is formed, composed almost entirely of addicts. The risk inherent in the heroin life also creates a situation of chaos for the postinitiate user. In addition, since using heroin is in itself disruptive, the user finds that few aspects of her/his life, drug-related or not, can be routinized.

Inundation by the addict life results from risk and chaos in the heroin world. Although he is referring to medical students, Broadhead's definition of inundation is useful in this context:

> By inundation, I mean an individual's life being flooded and dominated, at some times greater than others, by a substantively specific set of foci, concerns, and rounds of activities. It involves an absorption and encapsulation of an individual's general range of identities, interests, and activities into a far more substantively delimited and radically focused order of events and concerns that usually pivot around a single, all informing identity.[1]

Individual inundation by heroin occurs as a result of (1) the attempt to structure safe social networks in order to reduce risk factors and (2) the time consumed by heroin, a consequence of the riskiness of obtaining the drug and the ensuing chaos of the heroin world. In the following pages, I explore the dimensions of risk and chaos in the heroin world and describe how inundation results from these exigencies.

Risk

Each heroin-related activity—getting money (hustling), buying heroin, and fixing is inherently risky and disruptive. Moreover, the addict's recurring sickness adds a dimension of desperation to these activities that increases both risk and chaos. Because hustling activities are illegal in nature, they very often bring on the addict's arrest and incarceration. These activities become increasingly risky when the woman is sick because she tends then to be more desperate and careless and, therefore, attracts police.

Scoring heroin is risky for several reasons. First, the woman has to find a connection; if she is not able to contact anyone who she knows is selling drugs, she may have to ask around on the street. In the process, she may mistakenly approach an undercover policeman/woman or someone working for the police and be arrested. Even if she has a connection, an untrustworthy dealer may "burn" her—cut the heroin until it is extremely diluted with other substances—or even sell her a bag of something that is not heroin. (One woman, for example, complained that she had been sold Comet cleanser instead of heroin.) The woman also risks buying heroin that is "bunk" (poor quality) and does not affect her at all. And in buying the drugs, the woman associates for long periods of time with the dealer, and if s/he gets busted, everyone gets busted.[2]

Fixing, too, is risky: The addict can get abscesses or even hepatitis from a dirty needle. Several women had made small attempts to reduce this aspect of risk in heroin use. One woman, for example, used only purified water to "cook" her heroin. Another woman described her health conscious friend:

> She'd take $200 and walk down the street and blow $100 in the health food store all the time. She was a vegetarian, didn't eat sugar. Nothin'—no coffee, not one wrong thing. Just pure dates and dried fruit, just perfect. But she got so strung out! Just no head on her at all. But when it came to natural foods and all natural shit, she really got into it.

Men and women differ in their attitude toward risk. For male addicts, particularly at the beginning of their career with heroin or at the beginning of each new run, the daily overcoming of risk and chaos makes this life exciting and alluring.[3] When all the obstacles can be overcome—sickness, the law, finding a reliable connection with good heroin, having a place to fix, finding a vein, and finally, getting down—heroin is deemed a rewarding feeling for a hard half-day's work. There are few occupations or professions that offer the continuous satisfaction of accomplishment given tremendous odds. Whereas men often derive high status positions because of their willingness to engage in risk (for example, Feldman's "stand-up cat" and Sutter's "righteous dope fiend"), there are no such benefits for women;[4] furthermore, on a subjective level, women disdain the riskiness of the heroin lifestyle. It is not surprising that women derive no positive status from engaging in risk: The societal emphasis and expectation placed on *being* (a good mother, a good wife, a good girl) rather than *doing* and on passivity rather than activity limit women's ability to receive or experience positive feelings from risk.[5] Yet risk is a constant in the heroin lifestyle. All addicts are forced to live with it. If they can turn it into a positive value, so much the better, but for women this is not possible; instead, the risk simply results in a chaotic world.

Chaos

> To be a junkie is to live in a madhouse. Laws, police forces, armies, mobs of indignant citizenry crying mad dog. We are perhaps the weakest minority which ever existed; forced into poverty, filth, squalor, without even the protection of a legitimate ghetto. There was never a wandering Jew who wandered farther than a junkie, without hope. Always moving. Eventually, one must go where the junk is and one is never certain where the junk is, never sure that where the junk is is not the anteroom of the penitentiary.[6]

The activities that are part of the addict's life make establishing a structured routine nearly impossible. With the first event of the day—waking up sick—chaos begins. A woman who is desperate does not have the patience to think out her moves, to execute an ordered plan; therefore, her hustling patterns are both sporadic and chaotic. She may prostitute one day, boost the next, forge after that—

each without much plan or attention to detail. Her skills are never highly developed in any one occupation, so she hasn't one to fall back on. And what if she is too sick to hustle at all? Addicts don't have days off or holidays from their habits; when the rest of the city is celebrating (for example, on Thanksgiving), the addict's life may become more chaotic because hustling slows down (stores are closed). For the woman addict, then, work is inherently chaotic. This woman described getting caught up in the hustle and chaos of the heroin life:

> In the last couple of years, I've done some shitty things to people because I didn't want to be sick. But I wasn't sick this last time. I didn't need anything. It's just a habit—the habit of stealing and stuff—going through the thing of getting cash. A lot of people think it's the drugs, but it's not just the drugs that you are addicted to. It's the lifestyle that goes with it that is 90 percent of addiction. The heroin is just 10 percent, because there's a hell of a lot that goes with heroin addiction you go through, the whole ritual. It's like a ritual you have to go through to get that fix. You get yourself into a schedule. If you get a free fix, you don't know what fucking end is up. You don't know how it happened. Usually, you build yourself up for a fix by hustling. If you get a free fix, you're off kilter. You ask yourself, "Where did I leave off? What didn't I do today that I should have done?"

Scoring drugs is another aspect of the addict's life that can prove chaotic. Even if a woman has a reliable connection, the dealer may be arrested, thereby eliminating a heroin supply for all the customers. The connection's supply may dwindle due to conditions beyond control, or s/he may get low-quality heroin.[7] This woman's complaint was typical:

> I didn't have a wake-up this morning. I didn't have one yesterday because maybe our connection will be in town for an hour and it's all sold out.

Although numerous attempts have been made to quantitatively assess the amount of drugs used by an addict, the chaotic nature of the heroin life makes such calculations nearly impossible. Most women interviewed were not using a set amount each day; the amount depended upon the cost of the drugs, how much money they had at the time, the quantity of drugs available.

After the woman has bought drugs, she may not have anywhere to fix her heroin and have to find a shooting gallery, whose owner she pays (with money or heroin) to use the facilities. This is a much less frequent occurrence for women addicts than for men, since women generally have some kind of stable living arrangement and do not travel very far from their neighborhood to buy drugs.

Ultimately, finding a vein in which to inject the heroin may prove difficult. When asked about male/female physical differences among addicts, many women complained that, indeed, there was a big difference: Women have deeper veins, and it is, therefore, harder for them to fix heroin. The following excerpt from Goldman and Schiller exemplifies the difficulties any needle-using addict may have in fixing:

> Holding the syringe perpendicular, Lenny watches raptly as the first drop glistens at the top. He looks down at his arm.
> . . . This once-nice sinewy limb with that tattoo of the American eagle atop the bicep is now a ruined, festered crotch, a big black golf ball of infestation at the crack inside the elbow. The vein is ruined. Shooting six, eight, ten times a day inside the same vein has produced a hematoma, enormous, dangerous-looking. Lenny will have to shoot a smaller vein.
>
> Finally, he sees where it's possible to hit. The right hand is laid out flat on the table. He steadies his left arm, his shooting arm. . . . He starts to slide the needle into a vein about an inch behind his knuckles. Lenny isn't very steady. The first time he jabs only skin. He pulls back, sucks the needle clean and goes in again. This time he lances the vein, but when he starts to push the plunger he feels this sharp burning pain: "Shit, I've gone through. . . ."
>
> Lenny has pushed that needle clean through his vein. His hand oozes blood; pain nags at him. His head lolls down toward the table. His left hand trembles. "Terry, hit me!" He looks up. "Come on, man, please. . . ." Terry gives Lenny the garter end. He takes up the syringe. . . . There . . . oooooooh! A hit. A delicate column of blood starts to back up inside the plastic syringe.
>
> Lenny also sees the blood. He drops the garter and snatches the syringe from Terry. Squeezing down on the plunger hard, he empties the chamber, then starts to jack it full. The syringe is engorged with blood like a giant thermometer. He jacks at it another time when, suddenly, the Meth stuns him, and his head bobs down against the tabletop.[8]

The risk and chaos of the heroin world lead to social and time inundation and ultimately, to being locked into the addict world.

Social Inundation

Because the heroin routine and the activities connected with it are inherently risky (especially legally), addicts find it necessary to structure safe social networks. In order to avoid arrest by undercover "narcs" (narcotics officers), addicts are very careful in their associations to avoid individuals who are not known as "all right." The bulk of the people known as all right are other addicts. Additionally, because of the stigma of addiction and the outside world's deprecation of such a lifestyle, addicts tend to stay away from most "straights." The risk factor is multi-dimensional: While addicts feel that it is risky to associate with strangers because of the legal factor, straights feel that it is risky to associate with addicts because of their reputation for ripping off those around them, including loved ones, if necessary. Many women interviewed complained of the reputation addicts have acquired, and most stated that while they knew *others* who would rip off close friends and family, *they* themselves were of a different class and would never do such a thing. Indeed, according to these women, other addicts can and should be considered untrustworthy, but they had their standards. The effect, then, of the risk inherent in the heroin world is twofold. First, a separate social world is formed, composed almost exclusively of addicts, and the longer the addict is part of this social world, the more isolated from the nonaddict world she becomes. The entire world begins to look strung out.[9]

The addict social world is stratified much the same as the larger society of which it is part and product—on the basis of monetary gains and possessions. In this social world, the individual making the most money is generally the dealer.[10] Far fewer women deal than men, but a dealer's woman derives some of the monetary benefits from her man's profits. For women, deriving high status at all in the addict social world is difficult, and since the majority of addicted women prostitute at some point in their careers, they are automatically stigmatized—even in the addict social world. Nonetheless, women's status in the heroin world is determined by the amount of money available, because money directly determines behavior and consequently identification with the addict role.

Money determines the addict's behavior since the more money she has, the more room there is to be scrupulous or righteous. The addict at the top of the stratification system—the successful dealer or hustler—does not have to resort to those activities that characterize poorer addicts. In a practical sense, this may mean violating the two strongest codes that the women themselves advocated: taking care of their children and not stealing from close friends and family.

A code of ethics is, in fact, a part of the stratification system in the addict world. Theft, for example, is gradated. The more impersonal the target of stealing, the better; the closer to home, the worse the addict feels about it. While it is seen as all right, even courageous and bold, to steal from a large store or a person unknown to the addict, stealing from friends, family, and to a lesser extent, other addicts is not sanctioned.[11]

It is generally agreed that although a code of ethics once prevented inter-addict theft, it has disappeared: One addict will now steal from another. It is interesting to note that in the few armed robberies in which these women participated, the victim was another addict— usually a dealer.[12]

For the woman addict with children, as will be detailed later, unscrupulous behavior also takes the form of child neglect. In this sense, the woman addict is special, and her experience in the life is different, more pervasive than that of the man's. Society has vested responsibility for child raising in women, and when the heroin life becomes so chaotic that a woman cannot fulfill her responsibilities in this area, she is especially blamed for committing a crime with victims—her children.

In short, when heroin addiction becomes a crime with victims— family and friends who are ripped off or children who are neglected— the addict is especially remorseful. As the perpetrator of such crimes, she at once stigmatizes herself and is forced to regard her condition as an addict negatively; she sees herself as the stereotypical addict— the low-life, the rip-off, the junkie.

Resorting to unscrupulousness to support a habit is crucial to the identity of the woman addict. She generally experiences disgust with herself and recognizes and resigns herself to the status of junkie. In the same way that the woman who works (for example, as a prostitute) to get money for a fix recognizes that she has become an addict, the woman who finds herself stealing from family or close friends or neglecting her children also begins to see herself primarily as an addict. This has become her "master status."[13]

Crucial features of the addict stratification system are its temporariness and fluidity. The risk and chaos that characterize the heroin lifestyle prevent an individual from remaining at the top of the addict hierarchy for an extended period of time. Although dealers make the most money in the heroin world, the most successful dealers are not addicts, and those who are tend to "blow it" by using too much of the heroin they are selling. Very often, the dealer who is an addict becomes known to the police and consequently is busted periodically.[14] The situation of the dealer, then, is fluid: S/he constantly runs the risk of arrest and subsequent incarceration; such is the case with other illegal money-making endeavors. At one point, a woman may be "making it," and in another instant, she is incarcerated or ripped off—left with nothing.

Very often, women spoke of having lived with a dealer who was making lots of money. Once he was arrested, she was left to her own devices and quickly found herself very sick from withdrawal and out on the street turning $15 tricks and stealing from anyone who was proximate. Desperate behavior is even more likely to occur in those who are dealing because they build up such large habits that when the source of heroin is suddenly cut off, they experience more intense withdrawal symptoms than do addicts with smaller habits. The desperate addict then finds it necessary to exploit *any* source of money that is available—including loved ones; as Trocchi states:

> Thus, there is a confederacy amongst users, loose, hysterical, traitorous, unstable, a tolerance that comes from the knowledge that it is very possible to arrive at the point where it is necessary to lie and cheat and steal, even from the friend who gave one one's last fix.[15]

When the addict is back on her feet and has another source of income, she looks back on those activities with guilt and disdain. There is a general recognition in the drug world that this stratification is fluid and that all addicts have occupied or will occupy the bottom at one point or another; "looking down one's nose" is, therefore, not tolerated. In terms of status (as opposed to actual behavior), there is a certain equality among addicts. One woman said:

> Yeah, it does put everybody equal in a sense. Like I have a lot of friends who are girls, and who will go, "Well, I never had to go out and flatten my back out or nothin'. I never had to do that." You know, bullshit! Bullshit! You had to. You were sick. There's got to be a time where you had to wake up really sick and would go out and whore. I put it literally that way—whore. It depends on how the person is coming across to me, you know? Because I don't like that. It's not right to me to come across like

you are better than anybody. You're not, because using is using; there's no difference. The only difference is how you make your money or how you go about getting it. That's the only difference. But when it comes down to basics, it's all the same. You still stick the needle in your arm, your goal is the same— to get that fix and stick that needle in your arm and put that stuff in your veins.

The heroin world isolates itself from straights because they are suspect, considered intolerant and judgmental of the addict's situation, as this woman indicated:

I become very isolated from people. I don't like to see my friends because I don't like pity. I just don't want to see them. I don't want them to see me that way. Especially with this last episode I had with heroin, I was totally isolated from my friends and family. They always know when I'm on drugs because I don't communicate with them. The antisocial aspects of it or, I should say, the attitude you get from it—people aren't really your friends—that tends to make me want to isolate myself too.

In turn, addicts are excluded from the straight world because they, too, are suspect and stigmatized by images of unscrupulousness. One woman said:

When I'm hooked, I don't go around with squares because squares have this funny trip about dope fiends. If I'm hooked, they get to locking up their houses and watching their TV's and their stereos.

Thus, the woman addict finds herself both excluded from the straight world and inundated by the heroin world. She may taper the definition of herself as a junkie, redefining the term to mean simply one who is addicted and *not* a low-life or dog who will rip off family and friends. During a period when they were not down and out, many women were very careful to state that although they thought of themselves as junkies and outlaws due to their criminal activities to support their habits, they were not sleazy, had integrity, and would not rip off a friend; they were an addict of a higher class. Yet, the fluidity of the system is indicated by their own past accounts of unscrupulousness.

Risk, then, has the effect of structuring the heroin world so that it is made safer by excluding straights. Consequently, individual addicts tend to stick together, limit their friendship ties to other addicts who share their orientation and presumably, can safely be confided in. Straights are also excluded because addicts feel that they are suspicious of *all* addicts and label them as dangerous. Women begin to think of themselves exclusively as junkies because their entire world, activities, and social interactions consist of other addicts and heroin-related activities. As a result of this identification, it becomes increasingly more difficult to leave the addict world—both physically and psychologically.

It should be noted that although the addict social world is isolated and insulated, it cannot be characterized as possessing a sense of camaraderie. Many women were as suspicious of other addicts as the same women claimed "squares" were. These women fully understood the nature of the desperate addict's unscrupulousness and, consequently, had difficulty trusting anyone. As one woman put it:

> I really don't have any friends. To tell you the truth, I don't really consider anybody I know [to be] a friend. All they know is the connection, dope fiends, and junkies, and most of them will stab you in the back if you let them.

Distrust within the addict world and the feeling of being distrusted and uncomfortable around straights severely limits the woman addict's number of friends. Some women claimed they had many associates but no friends. Loneliness, then, is a consequence of having to minimize risk and of the resulting inundation by the heroin world.

Time Inundation

> When you are using, your whole world revolves around drugs, and when you are not using drugs and are working and all that, then your life revolves around everyday living. A simple thing like washing your car, going on picnics, going camping. . . . when you are using, there's no time for that.

The heroin life is so chaotic that heroin-related activities preoccupy the addict. She is too busy hustling, scoring, and administering heroin to have time to do what many women have called normal things. This woman illustrated the point:

> I can be sitting in the car waiting for someone to come down from copping and I can see two people coming down the street jogging and I kind of sit there and say, "Damn, I wish I could do that." But you can't 'cause the minute you wake up in the

morning, within a half an hour you got to get down or your nose is going to start running. And I just say to myself, "Gee, it would be so great to get up in the morning and throw on some shorts and go jogging and come home and eat a nice breakfast." I have to go fix, go find a connection. And if that person is out, you have to go find someone else who's got the good dope, and sometimes that takes two hours. Your whole day. I always felt when I was using that it would be nice just to do something very simple, like I say, jogging.

A large portion of the woman addict's activities focus around heroin in some way, leaving little time for fulfilling responsibilities in other areas. The addict who is financially bereft (a state that characterizes the lives of most street addicts) lives chaotically from fix to fix, hustling and scoring in between. The sum total of her existence is heroin—getting money, buying it, and then injecting it into her body for the ultimate purpose of getting well and possibly getting high. The pursuit of heroin is a driving, unending force for the woman who lives in a social world whose totality is heroin. The addict who is financially better off for a period of time is less desperate but still inundated by the heroin world; her life is less chaotic, but the risks are equal for the addict who is making it for a time and for one who is not.

The woman inundated by the heroin life knows pain, for by now the honeymoon has ended: She is hooked and senses that she no longer has the option to take or leave heroin. *It* is controlling *her* now; she is truly locked into her career as an addict. Her relationships with and responsibilities to children and lovers are most important to the woman addict. Evidence of her almost unwilling inundation by heroin is the transformation of these relationships while she is addicted. Her time is reduced to heroin-related activities, and consequently, she loses the option to hold up her end of a love relationship and most important, to mother. As one woman put it:

> Everything you are supposed to do today, you put off and you keep putting it off, putting off—hell with the phone bill, hell with the garbage bill, hell with the PG&E, hell with everything. Put off everything. It's beautiful. What else is there? Take a fix and go on the nod. Shoot. Wouldn't you like to spend your life sleeping?

Although it is possible for men to throw their entire focus on heroin and the heroin-related activities described earlier, women with children (as is the case of 70 percent in this sample) do not have such an option. The chaos and uncertainty of the addict lifestyle make even routine tasks of mothering extremely difficult: Generally, the woman who is addicted is either sick, busy hustling, or high. While she has neither the time nor the liberty to become completely engrossed in heroin, she must support her habit and hence take care of heroin-related business. This woman discussed her own special ability to fulfill her responsibilities to her children while contrasting her experience with that of other women:

> I feel that I have a lot of morals. I'm a junkie, but yet I have a reputation for always keeping a very nice house. My children are always clean. My children are always bathed. If there is a restaurant where the crowd hangs out at, like at Fort Help, there's a restaurant right across the street. And during the summer, my kids would go to the clinic sometimes; they would always go have something to eat. My kids are saying, "Ma, I want a cheeseburger." "Well, go get it." Other kids would go up to somebody and say, "Can I have a quarter?" If my kids ever begged, I think I would hit them on the face 'cause I don't want them kids ever begging. Then there are other dope fiend broads that keep their house like a pig pen. They don't even know where their kids are at, you know? "They are outside, I guess."

Women with children in our society are held responsible for their care; this is true for women in all categories—addicts as well as straights. Time inundation by heroin prevents women from taking care of business, fulfilling what is seen by them, their peers, and society as their main responsibility—their children. For this reason, Preble and Casey can define men "taking care of business" to be taking care of heroin-related activities, but when addicts who are mothers simply fulfill their responsibility to their heroin habit and neglect their children, they are seen as *not* taking care of business at all.

Conclusion

The chaos inherent in heroin addiction causes the woman addict to continuously go through changes. As already indicated, the tenuousness and illegality of heroin account for sudden upheavals in the structure of this world. A top connection may suddenly be arrested; there may be a shortage of good heroin; the police may at any time launch a campaign against prostitutes and addicts alike. Each addict is personally affected by the structural changes in this world: A heroin shortage means sustaining withdrawal symptoms for an extended time; police crackdowns mean a better chance of being arrested. These are the kinds of changes that the woman addict has to endure constantly, and with these changes, the woman not only gets sick for a longer duration and more intensely, but she also has to resort to more unscrupulous behavior to get money to buy heroin. If she is very sick from withdrawal, she not only becomes unscrupulous but often careless, thereby setting herself up for arrest and incarceration. Once incarcerated, her children will invariably be taken away, sometimes sent to family members but very often to institutions or foster homes. Finally, the chaos of the heroin world means the woman addict (and the man, too) is constantly balanced on the edge that divides maintaining herself in the heroin life from blowing it—being arrested. This balancing act can cause considerable tension for the woman, which, in turn, touches the lives of those who are close to her.

Risk, chaos, and inundation have a very significant impact on the woman addict's sense of identity, her identification with and immersion in the heroin life, and subsequently, her options for choosing other lifestyles. The risks in the heroin routine—from hustling to fixing—force addicts to insulate their world, and because of this insulation, they lose touch with individuals and social groups that are not part of the heroin world. Their own personal use of heroin and the narrow views of other addicts begin to dominate their thinking and perspective. Although many women complained that due to the risk involved in becoming close to addicts, they lacked solid friendships, their associations were composed almost wholly of other addicts. Fellow addicts may be threatening and untrustworthy, but it is worse to try to interact with squares who have no trust, understanding, or respect for addicts. Nonaddicts tend to lump them into a singular, stereotypical category of rip-offs and low-lifes.

The woman addict's self-respect is at least temporarily damaged when, due to the fluidity of the money-stratification system, she finds herself down and out, with no way to earn money legally. It is at this point that she becomes temporarily unscrupulous and may rip off a personal friend, even family. It is important to note that this unscrupulousness is *temporary* and that in some way, most addicts become unscrupulous in some form, at some point in their careers.

The most devastating aspect of the woman's time inundation by heroin is her inability to fulfill her mothering responsibilities. For women in the heroin world, unscrupulous behavior often includes child neglect.

It is the inability to take care of business (more than a fear of becoming otherwise unscrupulous and taking on the addict identity) that provides women with the impetus that is crucial for getting out of the heroin world. Yet, most women do not get out of the heroin world at this point; instead, they become more fully involved in the work world of the addicted woman and more fully immersed in the heroin life.

CHAPTER FIVE

Work

Sociologists generally treat work in occupational terms,[1] focusing on the broad range of jobs from professions to transient labor as work; yet, work is much broader and meaningful than a job, occupation, or profession and goes beyond traditional work settings. Analyses of work outside traditional settings can be an aid to understanding the work endeavor itself and the implications of work behavior. Criminologists, for example, have found it useful to study crime as work[2] in order to obtain descriptions of criminal behavior refreshingly devoid of psychopathological analysis. Looking at criminal and deviant activity as work also allows the sociologist to take a broader view of the concept of work. By taking work out of the traditional workplace and defining it as productive expenditure of energy, it is possible to apply concepts within the sociology of work to education, hobbies, and otherwise deviant occupations all located in social worlds not explicitly related to jobs. Miller compares deviant with nondeviant work:

> A fundamental assumption of this approach to deviance [deviance as work] is that deviant workers are primarily engaged in activities that yield monetary rewards that can be used to sustain their lifestyles. They are like all other workers in modern society who are also concerned with making a living. It may be true that there are other rewards and motivations associated with deviant work, but that does not make deviant work uniquely different from other types. Non-deviant persons also work for a variety of reasons. Work in modern society is, however, primarily an economic activity, whether the work role is popularly conceptualized as professional, non-professional, or deviant. Thus, although deviant workers differ from others with respect to the stigma that is attached to their work and themselves, the negative public image of these persons only complicates their work lives—it does not make their work categorically different from that of others.[3]

In this chapter, the term "work" is used to mean productive expenditure of energy in the pursuit of monetary gain, a concept that transcends traditional occupations and applies to the work—both legitimate and illegitimate—of women heroin addicts. I am specifically interested in one aspect of work—the relationship between work and identity.

Many students of occupations and professions have argued that individuals derive a sense of themselves, values, aspirations in general, and occupational socialization in particular from their work.[4] Moreover, individuals involved in deviant activity, particularly deviant work, tend to acquire deviant identities.[5] The heroin addict both works and regularly deviates from conventional and legal norms.[6] In this analysis, I address the problem of *how* identity is connected to work by showing how women addicts' identities shift from nondeviant to deviant, from straight to junkie simultaneous with the shift in their work patterns.

For the woman addict, the process of becoming a deviant and sustaining this identity is directly related to the methods she uses to support herself and her drug habit. It is crucial to note that it is not the use of heroin per se but her involvement in the social world of heroin buyers and sellers and her own copping (buying) activities that begin to mold her identity as an addict. More importantly, however, a woman's work patterns after becoming addicted have a central role in shaping her identity as an addict. The process of moving from legal to illegal work shifts her identity from that of an individual who makes a living within legitimate spheres to ultimate identity as an outlaw, which is tantamount to being an addict in an active sense. In analyzing this process, I begin by discussing the woman addict's involvement in legitimate work and then move on to illegal work, identity changes, and locking in.

Legitimate Work

Over half (53 percent) of the women in this population had held legitimate paying jobs at some early point in their heroin careers. Legitimate work and heroin use can be combined if a woman is very ambitious and conscientiously organizes her life and heroin use around her job. One woman who worked as a nurse talked about her heroin/work patterns:

> I used to work at the convalescent hospital. . . . I'd take one fix in the morning, and if I needed anything else while I was there, I

would go into the lady's room and do it. I was using about $60 worth of heroin every day. It was pretty easy to go to work and do that sort of thing. I was working a swing shift. There were only two other nurses and they worked at the same time and they didn't know what I was into.

If the addict is more immersed in work than in heroin use and if she has the control to accomplish it, restricting heroin use to weekends is the most effective way to combine heroin and work. In this way, the woman avoids taking on an addict identity. This woman noted:

I just sort of fell out of it [illegal work]. I don't know. Maybe I got tired of it. I remember some people saying, "Hey, you want to go to Salinas and work? Maybe you can get a job—a straight job." So, I thought I'd try that for awhile. I was still on probation from that strong-armed robbery, so I had to consider all this too. So, I did it—I went down to Salinas and I worked a straight job. I lived with people from the City and we were using. We'd come to the City on weekends to chippy. You know, that kind of thing. "We'll just chippy. *We're not really strung out. We're not junkies. We work.*"

For the habituated user, however, drug use can be extremely chaotic. Although the addict's need for heroin is predictable, buying and administering the drug are anything but routine. Finding a connection is often tenuous because dealers are often arrested and incarcerated. The price and quality of heroin are variable, which presents problems for the addict who is attempting to "get straight" (alleviate withdrawal symptoms without getting high) in order to function adequately. For the woman whose work requires regular and tightly structured hours and who is supervised closely, simultaneously working a legitimate job and maintaining a heroin habit is nearly impossible. Typical working hours are generally not consistent with the addict's fixing schedule, which is (not by choice) flexible due to the chaos of the heroin world. Therefore, the addict must often come to work before her morning fix, withdrawing, and sick. Furthermore, in order to administer her heroin, she has to go into the restroom or some secluded place several times during the day for prolonged periods. Since this is seen as rather unusual at the typical workplace, a supervised job is difficult. As one woman explained:

Working is hard because sometimes you are sick in the morning and you don't have the money to cop and you have to go to work sick. Or you wait to cop and come in late, so you keep losing jobs.

Another woman pointed out:

> When we came here, we started doing heroin again, and for about six months, we were both trying to work and keep things together. You just can't work and be addicted. It's very difficult, especially when you get to the point where you are going to the bathroom every two to three hours to fix.

When women addicts succeed in holding legitimate paying jobs, the job itself is often flexible and consistent with the heroin buying and using routine. In driving a cab, for example, the hours are flexible, and there is little direct supervision; moreover, the driver can leave work to buy drugs—another crucial aspect of the addict's day. As this woman noted:

> I've always maintained jobs and cab driving was perfect. There's a lot of junkie cab drivers. You are your own boss. You set your own hours. You are free to go cop any time you wish and you get paid daily in cash. It was perfect.

Jobs in notoriously quasi-legitimate spheres also allow a working addict to use heroin. While is it generally not sanctioned, addicts employed in sex occupations such as topless dancing, massage parlors, and the pornographic industry are able to both maintain a heroin habit and work. The locale of their jobs is convenient, as these places of business are generally located in high drug-using areas. Furthermore, if the woman's co-workers are heroin users, she has ready access to drugs when necessary.

In short, it is the structural aspects of certain jobs and workplaces that allow an addict to do her work while using heroin. These are jobs where the woman has control over her work, as in cab driving or is near a drug-purchasing area, as in topless dancing and massage parlor work. In fact, in some occupations, heroin use can facilitate retaining the job; for example, in those work situations where the woman must endure constant haranguing by customers, heroin use can make the job more bearable. Those women for whom heroin is an "upper" claimed that they could perform better as a cocktail waitress when using heroin. As this woman said:

> I was working as a cocktail waitress at Keystone, Berkeley. I would fix before I went to work, go in and hey, that was a heavy job 'cause there are a lot of people that come in, and I would

> have to fight my way through mobs of people with maybe a
> pitcher of beer and serve six people. And I was completely
> loaded the whole time. And I made more money than any of
> the other girls in tips and hustling. Dope kind of speeds me
> up, but then on my break, I would sit down and kind of nod.
> When I sit down, then I start nodding.

Although it is possible for a woman to maintain a heroin habit
while working a job with flexible hours and little supervision that enable buying and administering heroin during working hours, even
quasi-legitimate jobs that allow such a routine are rare.

The woman's physiological state plays an equally important role in
her ability to hold a legitimate job. The addict has three basic physiological states: straight or using just enough heroin to function otherwise normally; high or loaded from the effects of heroin; and sick or
withdrawing from lack of necessary heroin. When women were able
to retain work in legitimate spheres, they were generally coming to
work straight, not high or sick. When an addict is high, s/he often
goes on the nod, which is a form of temporary sleep. This woman
told about her mother, who was addicted and trying to hold down a
job:

> She just couldn't do it. I mean, she'd get loaded before work,
> and she'd get there and nod out at her desk. After just a
> couple of days of that, she got fired for going to sleep on the
> job.

Without heroin, an addict begins to experience withdrawal and
when sick from lack of heroin, s/he is irritable, fidgety, nervous, and
anything but attentive. Many women lost jobs because they went to
work in this condition. This woman reported:

> I tried to make it through the day without it [heroin], and you
> can't do that. I remember at work, I would be irritable and I
> was waiting for a promotion 'cause I was getting really high
> [advanced] at the phone company and I blew it. They tried to
> hang onto me too. They tried to help me with my problem.
> They really were pretty good people. But I lost the job.

Additionally, sick or high addicts tend to miss a disproportionate
amount of work. As this woman, an ex-postal employee, recalled:

> What happened at the post office was that I was strung out for
> about a year and a half. By the end of that year and a half, I

had to quit. I mean, my habit had become pretty large, and I couldn't handle both working and using. I ended up quitting. It's very hard to fire you at the post office, but they were doing all they could because I was starting to miss a lot of work. I think the last six months that I worked there, I probably was there about a third of the time.

It is very rare for a woman to find a job with structural conditions conducive to heroin use and to be organized and disciplined enough to go to work just straight rather than high or sick.

Although the majority of women in the population of addicts interviewed had held straight jobs and attempted to keep them after becoming addicted, most jobs were ultimately lost. The difficulty of working legitimate jobs is pointed out by O'Donnell:

> . . . the fact is that most addicts cannot afford to work at legitimate jobs. Whether because of minority group status, or lack of education, or failure to learn work skills or habits, or a devaluation of these skills and habits, or from more deep-seated personality problems, they do not have the capacity to hold high paying jobs. They can expect to earn less than their habit costs, so a job is not a solution. They need a hustle, an illegitimate but high-paying source of income. A further factor is that most regular jobs do not give them the time they need to make connections for drugs and the time and privacy for injecting them. Most addicts today use the intravenous route of injection, and this implies usually more than two shots per day. Those who do manage to hold down a legitimate job for any length of time while addicted are likely to have, in addition to fairly high pay and a fairly small intake, a stable source of drugs, which usually means a medical source, and use a long acting narcotic, by the oral or subcutaneous route.[7]

The loss of a job in particular and legitimate work in general is an important turning point for the woman addict. The imposition of a structured work routine, even when the woman cannot always comply, prevents her from going "full out" into heroin addiction and becoming inundated by the heroin lifestyle. As this woman said:

Q: Were you using at the time you were working?
A: Kind of. I was pretty busy. Sometimes I would get down (use heroin), but that job had me on my feet. If I had been really

strung out, I don't think I could have gone to work. But I wanted to keep my job, so I kept my habit down.

Another woman described her own pattern:

I worked here and I worked there. I'm using now. I'm using every single day. On my lunch hour, I'm boosting so I can have a fix when I get off work at night. It gets to the point where I can't hold a job. When that goes, I know that everything stable in life is going to go. As long as I keep some semblance of a job, it keeps my feet somewhere near the ground, but I know that once I give up that eight-hour gig that I am going to go totally. I know that in the back of my head! But when it comes to that, you can't keep the two. I'm too hooked.

Women who have not used illegal means to earn a living prior to heroin addiction usually resort to hustling when they have exhausted all other forms of money making. Waldorf describes hustling in this way:

Hustling . . . means any activity that utilizes guile or deceit to gain money. This may be either legal or illegal, but most often is illegal. The specific activities may range from selling drugs at a wholesale level to petty thievery.[8]

Getting into illegal work depends on both opportunity and "drift":[9] A woman's job is lost, she is sick, money is needed quickly, others are present to show her the ropes of illegal work. As this woman said:

My bank accounts were exhausted. I had no more money. Everything was sold. And that's when I committed my first burglary.

Many have noted that addiction and crime are concomitant.[10] For the woman who recognizes that she has a heroin habit, getting into illegal work takes the form of resignation or inevitability. As "Janet Clark" put it:

We were frantic for money naturally, to score with, and here was all this money to be made [by prostitution], and I thought that is what I'm going to be doing eventually anyway. And these are eventually my people [small time rackets] and for what am I holding back?[11]

In the following paragraphs, I describe the organizational patterns of women addicts' work, then I present a substantive analysis of their jobs.

Illegal Work

Odd Jobs versus Occupation

The interactionist school in the sociology of deviance has, in the tradition of the Chicago School, analyzed criminal behavior from an appreciative perspective.[12] Beginning with the work of Shaw and Sutherland, criminal activity was seen as a career in the same vein as traditional occupational careers.[13] Since the criminal's occupation is planned and carried out in a routinized, methodical fashion, the differences between legal and illegal occupations were considered to be in substance rather than form. The chaotic nature of heroin addiction, with its often erratic patterns of scoring drugs, makes it difficult for an addict to organize any part of her life. Nonetheless, some exceptional women addicts have what might be called an "occupation" by which they support themselves. They develop a routine around a particular form of work and have a set amount of money coming in from it every week. For example, a check forger explained her work routine:

> You just walk in and make a deposit and go to a different bank and then an hour or so later, do the same thing. Open an account, put a few dollars in and take some out. It gets to be quite a routine after awhile. You write down what banks you have been to and how frequently you've been to certain ones, so that you know which ones to avoid and so forth. It gets to be quite an intricate thing if you really get into forging checks. We'd go every day . . . go to two or three of them in about three-hours' time and have enough money.

Another woman noted:

> I made $200 a day boosting. It was easy. Take something out of a store, return it. I had a partner. Either I would go into the store and steal something and he would return it for the cash, or the other way around. We'd start at 9 A.M. and go 'till 9 P.M. We'd hit all the different shopping centers from Novato to Stanford. It was pretty good.

While some illegal work done by addicts is organized,[14] the majority is spontaneous and bears much more resemblance to the odd job than the occupation.[15] The following statement illustrates the odd-job work pattern of many women addicts:

> If I went into the Tenderloin or the Mission and, let's say, some guy came and asked me if I wanted a date, I would take that

date more than likely. If I was in a store and I found I could steal and I remember somebody wanted something, I would get it. You know, I don't even remember where the money was coming from [when I was hooked]. I can't really sit down and itemize or remember where all it did come from.

The illegal work choice of the woman addict resembles that of other workers in low socio-economic positions.[16] She is forced to choose her work—legal or illegal—in terms of the extrinsic values of simple economic gain, since she lacks the financial security needed to put intrinsic values of interest, challenge, and autonomy first.

The choice of illegal work is largely circumstantial. Many women become the apprentices of other women or men in their social circle; their training is informal—a "come-with-me" sort of education. Thus, learning the ropes and picking any particular hustle occur simultaneously, largely through convenient circumstances rather than elaborate planning and formal apprenticeship. As one woman described it:

Who taught me burglaries? A couple of different people. I went out with this one guy who did a lot of burglaries and I asked him, "Can I come along?" because I needed the money. I went along and helped him out and I did them with my husband, some girlfriends, different people.

Generally, women do not sit down and plan a hustling career as some individuals plan occupational careers; however, when women are not intensely sick from heroin withdrawal, they do determine rather rationally what is best for themselves at the time in a kind of cost/benefit analysis. A major priority is *safety*: Illegal work that nets the most money at the least risk is most desirable. This woman said:

You have to try different things in order to find out what suits you best. So, if you want to use drugs, you might as well find something that will work best for you. . . . [one in which] your chances for getting busted are less. . . . as long as I feel safe with what's happening, [the hustle] is okay for me.

Another variable in choosing illegal work is the *speed* with which money can be made; other important factors include the personal dimensions of the woman herself. She might take into account her skills at a particular trade and her moral feeling about the job. Her own sexuality may be an important variable in the choice of a job. The woman's age has bearing on her choice because it is related to such job qualifications as physical appearance and deftness. The woman's health is an especially important variable in her choice of work: The healthier the woman, the more selective she can be in choosing her work. If she is sick, the intensity of her withdrawal symptoms determines whether she will sacrifice such concerns as safety and morality in the kind of work she chooses. Above all, economic factors influence the woman addict's choice of work. The kind of work she chooses must net enough money to justify her time, risk, and often, the bending of her moral and sexual codes.

The women in this survey population had tried a variety of illegal jobs: auto theft (3 percent), burglary (18 percent), conning (6 percent), dealing drugs (61 percent), forgery (21 percent), pickpocketing (5 percent), pimping (1 percent), prostitution (60 percent), and shoplifting (28 percent). Although slightly more women in this study had used dealing than prostitution to earn their money, further investigation indicated that their dealing was quite sporadic and spouse-related. For the woman addict, prostitution is the most available and practiced means of illegal work; this finding is consistent with those of many researchers, who also found that the majority of women in their survey populations had supported their heroin habits primarily through prostitution.[17] Because prostitution is such an integral part of the lives of women addicts, it merits the extended discussion that follows.

Prostitution

Getting In

There are three basic avenues by which women get into prostitution: (1) independently—strictly for financial gain—either through conscious decision or by drifting into it; (2) through the encouragement of a boyfriend or spouse who sees prostitution as an activity from which they can both gain monetarily; and (3) against the wishes of spouse or boyfriend—to assert independence through money. I discuss each mode separately in the following paragraphs.

Most of the women who participated in this study had begun to use prostitution on their own—*strictly because they needed money.* Having a heroin habit to support is not always the major factor in turning to prostitution. As James has argued, the issues of causality in prostitution (prostitution causes heroin addiction or heroin addiction causes prostitution) have been belabored to little avail, and there is no conclusive evidence for either side of the issue.[18] Prostitution is often a faster way of making money than other work options open to women. As one woman explained:

> The first time I turned a trick, I wasn't using at the time. The guy I was with knew some girls—some working girls that had books—$100 tricks. That sounded a lot better to me than making $20 a day working in a restaurant. That's how I got into it. I needed the money.

Many women began to prostitute themselves because the financial need was present as well as the opportunity. Prostitution sometimes began in the neighborhood with boys who were personally known to the girl.[19] As this woman recalled:

> The first time I got paid for it, I was about 13 because this guy thought he was going to take me up into the hills and do it in the back seat. . . . so we get up there and he's trying his little things and everything and I say, "Gee, I really need some money." So, he gave me $20.

The basic need in this example was financial, and the opportunity conveniently presented itself. One woman said:

> After living in the neighborhood for such a long time, I knew a lot of people. A lot of guys that I used to see when I was up there, they used to try to get next to me. All the offers they used to make. . . . I used to turn them down. But when I got strung out, that was the time to . . . take 'em up on it.

For the white addict who entered the heroin world via the hippie trip, prostitution was often the natural progression from free love to paid love. As one woman who claimed that she hated prostitution but needed the money for college related:

> I nearly got sick to my stomach, but I used to do it because I had a goal in mind. I figured, "Why not? Instead of free fucking, why not get paid for it?"

In this case, the woman had been living in the Haight-Ashbury in a crash pad (she was a runaway) and had subscribed to the hippie ethic of casual sex. She became involved with heroin by using a variety of counterculture drugs and when she was addicted, saw that she could use her sexuality for financial gain. It wasn't until she was addicted and *had* to find some way to support herself that she considered prostitution.

Women who find themselves around prostitution, for whatever reason, may also consider trying it themselves; financial gain is *always* the reason. Another woman explained:

> When I was in Boston and I was young, I fell in with a lot of hookers. They were using, but I wasn't. They wanted to turn me out . . . and take me with them. Finally, one day I needed $20 or $30, and I got nothing out of it. It's just not my style.

Some women drifted into formal prostitution because the opportunity was present and again, there was financial need. As this woman said:

> I was separated from my husband and living in Hunters Point on Welfare. I had my children with me—my two children. I used to go down the street, down the hill to the store and a lot of sailors would come out from the Naval Shipyard and they would be whistling and all that bit and one thing led to another. I took 'em up on it, accepted their money. That's how it turned out, gradually—not realizing that I am putting a label on me, but that's how it turned out.

Whether the decision to enter prostitution was formal and well thought out, as in the two preceding examples, or followed the realization that it is possible to charge money for expected sexual favors or sexual favors from strangers or resulted from drifting after solicitation, it is clear that the basic motivation was financial.

Other women were encouraged to go into prostitution by male acquaintances who stood to gain financially from their earnings; as one woman recalled:

> When we were real young and hanging out with these black dudes, we wouldn't do nothing for them. We were virgins. They was already preparing us, getting us to learn how to make money. They'd be telling us for hours, "If you love your old man, you'd be out there making him some money."

This woman discussed being coaxed by a dishwasher in the restaurant where she was a cook:

> He took me out and we smoked a couple of joints of weed, drinking Hawaiian Punch 'til the late half of the night. He's showing me all the advantages of being a prostitute—nice

clothes and nice jewelry. All I have to do is go out and sell a little ass. Well, I said, "Okay." I finally gave in. But I already had my mind made up about that. So, that's the way I started in.

Very few women, however, described encounters with successful pimps; instead, most of the coaxing was done by small-time, would-be pimps. The women interviewed here were either too young to interest a successful pimp or too addicted to be able to put together the dress and demeanor of a higher-class prostitute, so they did not figure in the larger prostitution scene.

While many women are coaxed into prostitution by acquaintances who hope to gain by their work, the women who were seriously involved with men—either husband or boyfriends—claimed that they had to prostitute secretly because their old man did not approve and vetoed the idea. For these women, prostitution was used *in spite* of a lover's wishes in order to have money and be independent. Typically:

> I just needed money. When we were dealing, I was turning tricks, and my husband didn't know it. I just wanted money— my own pocket money. He wouldn't give me any.

Another woman described her relationship, which, like others where the man opposes prostitution by the woman, seems traditional in the sense that the man appears to have most of the power and seeks to control and dominate the woman by limiting her finances:

> I was turning tricks and he couldn't handle it. He was just like my husband now. We were fighting all the time. He didn't want me turning tricks. But I didn't want to live off him forever. I wanted to be able to try making some of my own money.

One woman said:

> I still feel guilty about that [prostitution] because it broke him up [her old man]. But, hey! I had no other choice but to do it. I did it when I had my kids. No one turned me out. I needed the money. In fact, I've always hooked alone. In fact, the men that I have had in my life always were dead set against it.

Addict-Prostitute Work Patterns

The woman addict who uses prostitution does so in patterns similar to her work at other jobs. Basically, because her life is chaotic, all work takes the form of odd jobs rather than occupations; she may burgle today, forge tomorrow, and prostitute next week—the variables are availability and skills. Prostitution is readily available to the woman addict, and the skills involved are maintaining at least a moderately attractive appearance and certainly a keen eye for risk and danger. Addict-prostitutes who become unattractive or unguarded in their approach to both tricks and cops, tend not to be successful.

Ironically, while practicing prostitution as an occupation is difficult for the addicted woman due to her heroin habit and concomitant problems, the ideal work routine is visualized as consistent and routine. The few women who considered themselves successful prostitutes talked about their routines; one woman said:

> I usually go downtown from 4 to 8 P.M. I go down to make my quota—about $150. If I make $100, I'm happy. I won't leave until I make at least $100 and then I'll leave. That's every day. I also have regulars. I just go down and call them. I have somebody coming over tonight.

The best routines are considered those where the woman is not physically on the street: She either has only regular customers or works out of a massage parlor. A woman with regular customers can possibly make $100 a day. She arranges to meet her customers by telephone, which is safe for both parties. Many women began relationships with regulars through work in massage parlors. One woman who prides herself on having only regulars presented a guideline for successful hooking:

> A hooker has got to be able to talk to people. She's got to be able to make a guy feel comfortable. Comfortable more than anything else. She's got to make him feel relaxed and appreciated. She's got to take him through a fantasy that he's very good sexually, try to build up his ego, and things like that. As for looking beautiful or pretty or anything like that, just build up what you *do* look like. If your thing is hippie, make yourself an interesting looking hippie. Make yourself an interesting looking whatever it is you are.

The element of *safety* is important for both the prostitute and her customer; the value the prostitute places on a regular routine, regular customers, and protected turf comes from knowing the hazards of chaotic streetwalking. Many women related "war stories" about their encounters with violent tricks or police. One woman reported the following incident as an example of the dangers of prostitution:

One time, my last date, I already had $150. And I was getting ready to go home. Then up comes this car, and, chesty me, stupid me, I just got in the car. The guy says, "How much?" and I says, "$30." Okay, car date. I jump in the back seat, took the money. He got in the back seat, pulls out an ice pick and puts it up against my neck, and he ripped me off completely. Took my money, the money he gave me plus me, you know? See, so you do take chances every time you do that. That's why I like my regulars. I know them.

The dangers and risk are two-sided. Part of the addict-prostitute's difficulty in maintaining a regular routine in prostitution is due to her heroin habit, which prevents her from consistently keeping her wits about her. On any given day, she might be unable to score and consequently be sick, desperate for a fix, and not looking her best. She cannot hold down routine work—whatever the type. It is in this state that the addict-prostitute occasionally rips off a trick. One woman talked about a particularly chaotic time in her life:

Business wasn't that good. I didn't like it. I was used to places where men would come to you. Business was so bad that occasionally I'd rip somebody off. One time, the john was in the shower. He had given me $50, and I took the other $50 in his pants.

Ripping off tricks can keep the addict-prostitute from having regular customers, from building up a clientele, thereby excluding her from safe prostitution, and without a regular clientele, the addict-prostitute's life becomes more chaotic and dangerous. One woman stressed the importance of establishing this regular clientele:

Like in the Tenderloin, it got very hot for awhile 'cause all the girls were ripping off tricks, and when the girls start ripping off tricks, that's when the cops start coming around. I don't rip off tricks because I want them to be regular customers. I have ripped off tricks, you know, tricks that were drunker than drunk and wouldn't know anyway—or weren't regular people who came around the Tenderloin.

Another woman too old to prostitute now but similarly inclined said:

I've got tricks that give me money, and I haven't seen them in six months. Like Christmas, I got $500 just from my tricks, and some of them I haven't seen in six or seven months because I don't turn tricks now. Very, very seldom. I might turn two tricks every six months, but I was good to them when I was working. I didn't let myself go like a lot of the girls do. I never stole a nickle from them ever. I was always there when I said I was going to be there, so I can go to them any time and get $20 or $30 if they have it. It's good to do that.

Prostitution is an odd job fraught with dangers and risks for the woman addict. In an attempt to reduce these dangers, some women work with and for men; however, once a woman relinquishes her status as a free agent, she tends to have to work much harder than her man—whether he is formally her pimp or her lover. In these situations, prostitution may become safer, but the addict-prostitute works longer hours and makes less money. As one woman said:

> When we got so hot in Oakland, when he and I got so hot, I was coming out and hustling on the street to make money. I had to make $250 for him and $250 for me. I had to make $500 a day on the street every day of the week.

Another woman described how her man forced her to shoot Ritalins:

> I didn't like Ritalins, but he wanted me on them so I would go out and work the streets. I had him with me for protection—I don't like being alone. I was giving him my money, and he'd get me high when I wanted. It didn't last. It was nice at first and then he started pulling shit. He'd say, "If you don't bring in $200–$300, I'm going to beat the shit out of you and you won't get fixed."

The threat of being arrested by an undercover policeman posing as a trick, a trick who is a rip-off, and/or an exploitative pimp make prostitution risky and dangerous for the woman addict.

Women Addicts' Ranking in the World of Prostitution

The world of prostitution has its own stratification system; it is based, like the larger society of which it is a product, on economics. Simply put, the higher-paid prostitute ranks at the top of the stratification system, and the lower-paid neighborhood streetwalker ranks at the bottom. One woman described the fate of a friend who became a streetwalker:

> She went off the deep end right away. I was working up there for a long time, and I don't have *no* trouble—nothing wrong with me. The first minute she gets here, she goes off with the

first pimp she sees. . . . next thing you know, she's out in the open on MacArthur Boulevard. . . . all this shit.

In the world of prostitution, quality is determined by place of solicitation, clientele, and the appearance of the prostitute herself. Since prostitution is a fee-for-service arrangement, the higher-quality prostitute can charge more than the lower-quality prostitute. The prostitute who works strictly out of a book (a call girl) has more prestige than the prostitute who works in expensive hotels; the streetwalker is the lowest, with the downtown-hotel streetwalker ranking above those women who solicit in ghetto neighborhoods. On this basis, there is a racial discrimination within the world of prostitution. As this black woman related:

> I must be prejudiced or something, but I always would rather do something with a Caucasian. They don't talk that $10–$15 stuff. I did one and I'd get $25–$30 for just one. When I was dealing with blacks, my own race, it was $15 or $20, which wasn't that far off from $25, but if I just needed it, I would take it. I have taken it, but $10 is no good. . . . no good.

Call girls often have a clientele of high-status men whose names are procured through business associates or colleagues. As one woman explained:

> I've got regulars now. They just call me up and I go down or they come over. And I've got a couple. One's a senator who I won't mention, and another guy is a big-time dude. I know what he is. He's Japanese. $300 a trick for 15 minutes.

The prostitute who works the downtown hotel might be dated by conventioneers or other out-of-town, middle-class men. This is less financially lucrative than the call girl's clientele but preferable to working one's own neighborhood. The neighborhood where the woman lives tends to attract other drug users and lower-class ghetto dwellers. This kind of john is far less desirable than the other two types mentioned.

> The streets is a whole different trip in San Francisco—different than working a book. A book means phone numbers. The clientele is different with books—you know them. They don't want anybody to know. They're nicer. You don't have to worry about getting your ass kicked or getting the money from them. You don't have to ask for the money first like you do on the street here.

The prostitute's appearance is most important, since she is trying to attract customers. The less she looks like the stereotypical version of the prostitute, the more she will be paid. The call girl, as exemplified by Jane Fonda in *Klute*, would not be mistaken for a prostitute, who is often heavily made up and wears skimpy clothing. One woman described the different modes of appearance in this way:

> Some of those girls in Oakland are righteous thugs. . . . standin' on the street corner, leanin' up against a post in body suits and jackets and boots and black stockings. That's it. They don't play that in Chicago where I worked. I was wearin' evening gowns and shit. You don't walk around in no body suits, standin' on no street corners.

The addict, especially the white woman, often begins her activities in prostitution as a high-ranking prostitute; she may get customers from her work in massage parlors or from contacts with other prostitutes with books. All goes relatively well for her as long as she can keep it together, keep up her appearance, work respectable areas. The problem for the *addict*-prostitute is that her addiction eventually prevents her from keeping it together: Her appearance becomes slovenly or she works in an indiscreet manner, thereby attracting police. As one woman noted:

> I wanted to keep it as discreet as possible. I wasn't standing out there talking to the other girls when I would go out. And I wouldn't go out in jeans. I seen all kinds of whores comin' through that jailhouse tank, and you should see them. . . . If I knew I was goin' out, I would try to make myself appealing, even if I had to do that and come back and take what I got on off and put on some dirty clothes.

In addition to neglecting her appearance, the addict-prostitute begins to work neighborhoods where her connection resides; in this way, she is never geographically too far from a fix. In these neighborhoods, however, only the low-paying johns will solicit her.

Possibly the most important factor in the addict-prostitute's slippage is the john's knowledge of her habit and the frequency with which she experiences withdrawal symptoms. When she is sick, the addict will take less money for a date. As one woman said:

> After I had been recognized as using drugs, guys wouldn't offer me $25 or $50 or $35. They broke it all the way down to $15 or $10. After things had gotten so hard, well, I'd just have

to take it and drop the old pride. I knew something wasn't right. That was just about it. After feeling like you are about to lose your womanhood, it's time to slow down or quit or do something.

Another woman remarked:

It's a big difference. Like if somebody came up and offered me $20 when I wasn't hooked, I'd say, "Get lost." But when I was hooked, $20 would get me a fix. That's the difference. That's why in the Tenderloin, people would come up and say "$10," and they can get away with it with some bitches. They get so hooked, they'll take $5 or $10.

Because more johns know that addict-prostitutes will take less money, some women try to keep their addiction a secret by keeping themselves together:

If you are hooking and if you've got a habit . . . you don't make it any secret that you are a prostitute. You dress up nice, but not too nice, because if you dress up too nice, you'll scare them away because they'll think you want too much money. They always try to hustle you down to $15 or $10 because they figure you are strung out and you need the money quick. And they try to take advantage of that. You have to give them the idea that you're *not* strung out, that you don't use at all, and that you're just out there hustling because you need rent money or something. That you need the money, but you're not desperate at the moment. . . . And usually, you'll get the money you need.

The addict-prostitute ultimately falls into the category that Goode describes in these terms:

There are also what might be called the down and out, hand-to-mouth prostitutes—the "losers" of the profession. The woman who drifts from man to man, and hustles between men. Who wanders in and out of "the life" without accumulating any capital, without building up a list of customers or contacts, or acquiring any skills or knowledge concerning what they do—sporadically—for a living. At every activity, every profession, every endeavor, some people are simply more successful than others. Many women are *unsuccessful* prostitutes. They don't have the ambition or the motivation—or the stomach—to work day in and day out, full-time, full-tilt, at a job that is unappealing to them. When an opportunity comes along, they quit. Instead of turning five or ten tricks a day, they might turn two or three. Instead of walking the streets five, six, or seven days a week, they will walk two or three. They use prostitution just to *get by*, to tide them over until something better comes along, until they meet a man they like, until they earn a little money to coast for awhile.[20]

Going through Changes

Women addicts become involved in illegal work primarily because they need more money than can be earned in low-paying occupations for which they are qualified. The shift from legal work or traditional roles (such as mothering) to active illegal work is an important transition for the addict:

Q: At what point did you begin to think of yourself as an addict?
A: Mostly when I started selling drugs. I used to call myself a "dope fiend." I especially thought of myself as a dope fiend when I was out selling my body and things like that—*just for money to buy drugs.*

The illegality of the work and the fact that it is used in pursuit of money for drugs are the most important aspects in the relationship between illegal work and changes in identity. The woman begins to see herself as both a junkie and an outlaw because she is using illegal work to obtain drugs.[21] The motivating force behind the woman's involvement in illegal work is her heroin habit; it is withdrawal or fear of withdrawal that gives her the drive to hustle—day in and day out with few breaks and no vacations. In fact, when addicts stop using heroin and cease to experience regular withdrawal symptoms, they often feel that they no longer have the heart to hustle. This woman said:

> . . . like I was telling my ex-husband the other day, "If you came over here with a bunch of checks and it was a sure thing where I knew I could go out there and get about $3,000, I don't know if I would do it or not." I don't think I have the heart to do it anymore. Being strung out gives you a drive that you are just going to go out there and do it. You could go to the moon.

The woman addict is *first* a junkie who becomes an outlaw in pursuit of her heroin; she sees herself as less morally reprehensible than other deviant workers because she has less choice than those who are not addicted. This addict-prostitute who, like most other women addicts, did not like her work looked askance at nonaddicted prostitutes:

> I don't think I could dig being looked at like that. So, if I do sell my body, I want to be respected for it. I'm not out there doing it because I get off doing it *but because I need the money.* Some chicks are out there just doing it for fun. I got a monkey on *my* back.

The woman addict, therefore, derives her identity as an addict (most women called themselves "junkies" or "dope fiends") from her involvement in illegal work. At the same time that she shifts from straight to junkie, the woman addict becomes a deviant worker—but this identity is secondary: First, she is a junkie who needs to hustle because she has a habit. She, therefore, attaches little seriousness, commitment, or personal involvement to her work, treating it as an odd job, and thus, is able to rise above the denigrations to which women addicts and outlaws are subjected. Like the menial laborer who works for the money and finds his/her real self elsewhere, the woman addict sees her addiction as responsible for thrusting her into illegal work but excuses her activities as heroin-caused. It is not heroin addiction per se that she finds questionable but the things it forces her to do. As Duster notes:

> It is critical that one understand the way in which the (ex) addict makes a separation between the moral meanings of drug use and the moral meaning of other illegal activity. He does not regard the consumption of morphine or heroin itself with moral approbation; but rather it is those things which addiction to drugs drives one to that he regards as morally reprehensible.[22]

Locking In

Although the woman addict sees herself primarily as an addict who is forced to do illegal work to support her habit, her social identities as both junkie and outlaw lock her into the heroin world. As a junkie, she must confront herself with the "once a junkie, always a junkie" prophecy; as an outlaw, she must confront the world.

The woman derives her identity from her work in illegal activities and inundation by the heroin world. She finds that she is locked into this world when she fails upon attempting to get out (become opiate-free). With each subsequent attempt and failure, she begins to believe more strongly that she will, indeed, always be a junkie. This is the psychological aspect of her imprisonment in the heroin world. One 47-year-old woman stated:

> I'm a very ambitious person and I make friends easily. I like to work. I like to go to school. I wanted to be a nurse. I wanted to go to City College. I wanted to do all these things. . . . but once you are a dope fiend, you lose all your lights. Yeah, I blew my life. I would have been doing something really worthwhile had I not gone off into heroin. Now, I can't get out. I'll never get out.

As an outlaw, the woman addict rarely escapes detection, arrest, and incarceration at some point during her career (78 percent of the women had done some time in jail or prison). Once the woman has been incarcerated and officially labeled a criminal, she finds it more and more difficult to break out of illegal work and find a legal occupation. This 43-year-old woman said:

> I have great work potential and skills. When I was in CRC, I worked in the office. I was head clerk and typist in the office. I did all the papers for all the police departments and everything. I did all the release papers and everything. All of that and I loved it. I loved it! When I came home from CRC, I honestly tried to get a job. I sent resumes to every ad in the paper—every single ad. I went on five or six interviews. I didn't get a job. If I had gotten a job, I think I might not have been into it as much as I'm into it now. Might have chippied, but I wouldn't have been into it as much. Okay, this is the thing that stopped me. When they asked me, "When was your last job?" I said, "14 years ago." I'm not going to tell them I picked up my typing speed again in CRC. I'm not going to tell them that. Fourteen years ago was my last [real] job. And then they say, "I'm sorry, but we want someone that has recent. . . ." I couldn't get a job.[23]

Conclusion

By giving an economic interpretation to her work, the woman addict who has many odd jobs sees herself as "in it" for the money to pay for heroin. She defines herself as a person with basically straight values who due to an oppressive habit has to work at many kinds of deviant jobs. As far as she is concerned, the work is not who she *really* is, and, therefore, she should not be defined in terms of any job she may have at a given time. The label "junkie" is much more in keeping with her sense of self than an identity based on a particular type of criminal work.

Although the woman addict does not derive her identity from any one kind of work, her identity as a junkie is derived primarily from involvement in criminal work. Many women claimed that it was when they realized that they had committed crimes in order to get money for heroin that they began to see themselves as a junkie rather than as just a casual drug user. The inverse is also true: Those women who resist being labeled as junkies also resist becoming involved in criminal work, asserting that if they can stay away from criminal activities, they can stay away from the totality of the heroin world.

The woman addict's heroin-related work activities lead her to identify with the social world of addiction. This identification occurs when the addict goes to *work* to support her heroin habit. Once the connection between work and identity has been made and the woman has accepted the label of addict, junkie, or dope fiend as central to her person in whatever context, she is essentially locked into the heroin world.

A heroin habit becomes so difficult to maintain that most women ultimately want out. They often express their desire to leave the heroin world by attacking the basis of their identity: addiction (being a junkie) and work (being an outlaw). This woman illustrated the point:

> Being a junkie embarrasses me. I hate it and I don't want to be a junkie. I don't want to be known as one. I want to get a good job. One that I really like—that I really love. And move into a nice apartment and have a real good relationship with my old man.

When women attempt to make the transition out of the heroin life, their first goal is to secure a legitimate job. Most women see the shift to legal work as crucial in restructuring their lives and identities as nonjunkies. As one woman said:

> At first, when I go back to the working life, it's kind of hard for me to get into the people again, but after I've been working there for two weeks maybe—I'm happy about this part, because I can just block out the dope scene world and just jump into their world again after I've been in there a few times. I'd really rather have it that way.

Another woman stressed the importance of work in relation to cleaning up and feelings of self-worth.

> The reason I could clean up was because I was introduced to a whole new lifestyle. It was the help of another person who was into something that I wasn't. And the main thing is the feeling you have about yourself. If you start feeling a little proud about yourself, you have self-worth. When I would meet people, even before I told them my name, I told them, "I have a job." I was so goddamned proud—me, man, I'm workin'! Most people do have a job, but to me—it was phenomenal. Things like that made me feel good about myself. Made me feel like I liked myself and most dope fiends don't.

Women often encounter problems in attempting to do legitimate work; the stigma of having been an ex-convict, often an ex-prostitute, and an ex-addict initially prevents them from being hired. In fact, women experience the stigma of addiction more intensely than do men. A woman who has been a convicted criminal and/or addict is considered much more deviant than a man with the same record. Thus, after the woman has been involved in illegal work, her options begin to narrow at a faster and more irreversible rate than a man's; she is being punished more severely for trespassing on society's values than is her male counterpart. When she begins to have problems in taking care of the business of mothering, her options will narrow even further.

Even if a woman can get legitimate work after having been involved in heroin, her low-educational level and lack of job skills force her into menial labor, which she finds boring and financially unrewarding. As a result, securing and keeping a legitimate job is quite difficult. As long as a woman can maintain a job and remain opiate-free, she can make it outside the heroin world. When jobs are lost or impossible to get, she feels that she has failed and frequently turns to heroin. The cycle of addiction and illegal work begins again.

CHAPTER SIX

Difficulties in Taking Care of Business

The career of the woman addict involves risk, chaos, and ultimate inundation by the world of heroin. Participating in the heroin life means relinquishing other activities and, consequently, life options not related to heroin procurement and use. The woman who becomes an addict generally had little focus and commitment in her life prior to addiction. Heroin, in fact, provides her with a needed focal point as well as excitement and (albeit involuntary at times) commitment. Although the woman's career in addiction begins with excitement and expanded options, her options begin to narrow with time. The chaos and cost of the heroin life force her into illegal work and, ultimately, into dealings with the criminal justice system. Once involved with the law, her occupational options outside the heroin life are reduced; equally if not more importantly, inundation by the heroin world threatens the life option she deems most valuable: her family.

Lovers

"When drugs come into the picture, love flies out the window."

Although heroin can provide a common focus, the nature of the heroin life ultimately undermines love relationships. In the following sections, I examine relationships gaining a focus through heroin, their eventual undermining, and finally, how undermining contributes to a narrowing of options for the woman.

Heroin as Providing a Focus

The characteristic inundation by the heroin life often provides focus in a love relationship; it is the commonality shared by a couple, the direction in their relationship, the basis of understanding between them. Heroin is not unlike a shared occupation or profession, common interest in a hobby or sport, or the joint effort and interest in building a family and raising children.

While male addicts often prefer to have spouses or old ladies who are not addicts, such is rarely the case among women. Even if they had not entered the heroin world through a man, the women interviewed in this study who were part of a love relationship usually had mates who were either addicts or ex-addicts; the couple could, therefore, be categorized as an addict-couple. Since heroin, unlike most occupations or hobbies, is a full-time endeavor, the addicted couple tends to spend a great deal of time together. Many addicted couples have virtually a 24-hour relationship, doing everything together—hustling, scoring, fixing, sleeping, and eating.

Sexuality is, however, one aspect of a love relationship that is nearly omitted in the case of the typical addict-couple.[1] Due to the effects of heroin, very often the man cannot perform sexually and/or does not care about sex. The same is true for the woman:

> When I was using heroin, I found that I had very little interest in sex. I mean, sex was something I did for money. Sex was something I had very low interest in. Unless I had a strong interest in some other person, well, even then sex was secondary. Drugs took precedence over anything else. . . . sex wasn't important to my old man either. I've discovered this is true of most addicts. Sex was kind of a secondary thing.

The woman is often nonorgasmic while addicted, but even if she has some sexual desire, sex is too much work to be rewarding:

> But then it got to the point where you don't need to have sex. Everyone finally came to the realization that, shit, it took ten hours to have an orgasm and then it was so light, it wasn't worth the energy you had to put out. By the time you had worked up to have an orgasm, you needed to get off again on dope because you weren't that high anymore. So, you didn't get to enjoy the high, so it was just like having to put out—it was like, "forget it." Everyone just turned off.

Many women claimed that the fixing routine, particularly when their partner "hit" them (administered the heroin), replaced intercourse.

> Sex is not important. Your body doesn't feel any desire for sex,

and to me, dope seems to take the place of sex. So, my husband hits me. It takes the place of sex subconsciously.

The sensuality and sharing aspects of doing heroin together are another replacement for sexual intercourse. As this woman put it:

My interest in sex wasn't as great because I just felt like fixing was such a. . . . I just felt so good. And there's a kind of an affinity between you and your old man when you are fixing together. That you are on the same high, you both feel the same way. It's a very secure kind of feeling that I didn't need to enhance by fucking.

Above all, sexual intercourse is missed by neither partner. Consequently, the couple who genuinely cares for each other is platonically involved in all activities and tends to develop a brother-sisterlike partnership where there is interdependency with regard to earning money and often protection for the woman.[2] The partnership between addicts can become a habit, just like their joint addiction to heroin:

I don't know. I think that if the man and the woman are both strung out—if they don't really have a relationship, it's just a habit. They're shooting partners, they're crime partners, and that's about it. I think that if they were both to clean up, they'd realize that habit.

Drugs gradually come to replace all other aspects of the addict-couple's relationship, so that even an otherwise expired relationship can remain intact. Just as heroin often masks physiological disease symptoms, it can cover up those aspects of a love relationship that would be intolerable without heroin. It is only when one or both "cleans up" that they realize their relationship has been based exclusively on heroin; as one woman explained:

We stuck together when we were using, but when I got on methadone and he wasn't on it, it seemed like I was kind of out of the picture. Like he'd go in the bathroom and fix his drugs, and I just didn't feel like we were communicating. He was doing one thing and I was doing another.

Heroin as Undermining

Although a partnership can be ideal for the addict-couple, drugs ultimately undermine relationships in three ways: heroin becomes the focal point of the relationship and erodes other aspects of affection or mutuality; the heroin life disrupts traditional sex role delineation to the dissatisfaction of the couple; and unscrupulousness and money problems cause nearly constant bickering.

As mentioned before, the addict high on heroin doesn't really care about the activities of people around her/him. Sexuality is impaired due to this inability to relate intensely to another person. The focus that heroin provides for the couple is strictly functional, based on mutual pursuit and use of heroin; affection and emotional attachment nearly always suffer.

Occupational options in the heroin life often allow the woman to work when the man cannot, since she has the option to prostitute (which few men have).[3] Therefore, even if the man in a relationship does not pimp his woman, she will often have to assume the responsibility of earning money for both their habits through prostitution. One woman related:

> Women bear the whole brunt of the load. You can believe that. Anytime you see a woman with a man and they got a habit, you can believe she's got to carry the load because she's the one who can go out there and literally "sell her ass." A man can't do it and he sits back and waits. . . . There is very little a man can do, very little. Nowadays, all these games that used to be played—boosting, bunco, and all that—that's all passe, man. There's articles and stuff about it in every magazine from end to end. Everybody's so down on it. Unless you go into the big time and if you go in for that, you are not going to be using no stuff. You can believe what I'm telling you. But it's the woman right out there on the street, today, tonight, where I go, where I stand—she's the one taking the chances. She's the one that gets kicked in the ass.

Such an arrangement ultimately proves unsatisfactory to both partners. Thus, the second undermining aspect is the disruption of traditional sex roles that results from differential earning power in the heroin life, a situation is not unlike those described by Rubin in working-class marriages,[4] Liebow in lower-class black marriages,[5] and Sackman in addict relationships.[6] In each case, the man begins to resent his wife's or woman's earning power, especially if it is greater than his own. As Rubin notes:

> Indeed, it is just this issue of her [the wife's] independence that is a source of conflict in some of the marriages where

> women work. . . . in well over one third of the families, husbands complain that their working wives "are getting too independent."[7]

As noted by Komarovsky in regard to Ivy League men, there is confusion and discomfort when "the ideological supports for the traditional sex role differentiation in marriage are weakening, but the emotional allegiance to the modified traditional pattern is still strong."[8] The addicted man in an economically dependent situation often becomes resentful and attempts to assert his power through violence directed at his mate. As one woman related:

> I used to come home [from a day of prostitution], and he's [her spouse] laying around, waiting for me to give him the money so we can cop [buy heroin]. We'd get the stuff and he'd try to short me saying, "I've got a bigger habit," and shit like that. I just wasn't going for it. I mean, it was *me* that was out on the street all day while he was laying around. I'd get pissed and then he'd just blow it . . . knock me around and stuff. One time, he nearly put me in the hospital.

The woman, who usually does not like her work, resents such violence and feels doubly exploited if her man is not working. Since it is commonly assumed that the major breadwinner will have the privilege of dispensing the heroin, the woman is especially bitter if she earns the money and her man insists not only on dividing the heroin but on giving her a smaller portion!

The unscrupulousness that periodically characterizes nearly all addicts usually enters the addict-couple's relationship and becomes a third source of undermining. In times of withdrawal sickness, one addict may rip off the other's money, heroin supply or pawn the others belongings; one addict may gain access to heroin without splitting it with the other, which is tantamount to sexual betrayal.

An unequal division of labor, heroin, and money often leads to women's resentment and bitterness; sex role disruption can lead to men's violence. Both ultimately undermine a love relationship. There are disagreements over how money is to be earned, how heroin is to be divided, and ultimately, how money in general is to be spent. As this woman said:

> We just fought a lot about who was getting more (drugs). Oh, I don't know, it happens with every relationship I have. We bitch about who is getting the most dope. It's what starts happening. When I left my ex–old man . . . I knew it was me who

was doing the bitching because he had most of the money.
Usually, whoever is making most of the money figures they are
entitled to more dope. If I was making more money, I'd figure I
was entitled to more of the dope. And if somebody starts
bitching, things get really fucked up. So, it works both ways. It
depends on who is making the most money. It's kind of hard
to keep a relationship going when you are strung out. A lot of
times we sat and talked about, you know, things that we want,
what we should be doing and we're not doing with our money,
and the reason you ran out of money is because of dope. Yeah,
and you always blame it on each other. You can't blame it on
the heroin, you know? (laughing) You got to blame it on each
other.

Women sometimes regret what they see as their partner's excessive
use of money for drugs. Occasionally, the impetus for beginning heroin use had been to get a share of the substance for which all the family money was being spent—drugs. Later, women have similar concerns over how money is spent but are more often concerned about
their children and living situation. This woman said:

Well, right now I've been really uptight with him because I feel
he is spending too much money on heroin. I wish that right
now we weren't using as much as we are, because he makes
money and right away wants to spend it on dope, whereas I
would rather use it for other things it should be used for—the
house, our kids, you know.

There is nearly constant arguing over heroin and money, and as a
consequence, most relationships involving addict-couples cannot be
sustained. According to one woman interviewed:

I think drugs broke my husband and I up. I think when drugs
came into the picture we were still very much in love, but the
drug came in and I lost a lot of respect for him 'cause I kind of
straightened my act up and I see him now laying there sick
and I say, "How stupid can this asshole be?" Like right now,
he's staying on my couch. He hasn't got a damned penny in
his pocket. He's got no respect for himself. I've lost respect for
him, and I feel that as long as the two people are into shooting, they're both sick, and they're hanging onto each other for
strength.

The failure of love relationships to endure within the heroin life and the deleterious effect of this life on the health and appearance of the woman addict reduce her options to fulfill a traditional marital role. Although a few men find it advantageous to have a dope fiend old lady because of her ability to prostitute and bring in money, a woman who has been in the life for a period of time is seen as undesirable to men because of her history of addiction. Similarly, women very often see relationships with addicted men as undesirable because of their past history of addiction and all the ramifications.

Many women become bitter toward men because they feel they have been exploited and battered. Some women find love relationships with other women more satisfactory. There is less violence in such relationships and more egalitarianism. As this woman says:

> Men are, they get, dependent on a woman and they get used to that and they get to the point where they don't want to go out and hustle. And you not only have to carry your weight but their weight, pay the rent, buy the food, the clothes, and take care of the kid. So, after I broke up with my husband when I was 15, I had it with men. I had a lot of old ladies but not a man. A woman will hustle right along side of you, where a man will hustle at first 'til he gets hooked. And then he'll want you to make all the money, and if you don't, you'll get your ass kicked.

The inability to sustain a love relationship, whether or not as a result of the woman's own bitterness and resentment, further narrows the woman's options. Victimized and exploited by men, she may no longer desire to establish traditional marital or quasi-marital relationships with men—one of the few options that was open to her at the outset.

Mothers

> I don't like the lifestyle at all. I mean, I have fun when I'm running out there, but I miss my kid too much. Like, if I didn't have my kid, I wouldn't even worry about it. It wouldn't bother me at all. I keep on doing what I'm doing 'cause I have fun. But I got my kid. He tells me, "Mama, when are you going to take me home with you for good?" Everytime I hear shit like that, I just snap inside. It really breaks me up.

Seventy percent of the women interviewed in this study were mothers; they consistently expressed concern, care, and often, guilt about their role as mothers and the well-being of their children. Moreover, they seemed to have accepted social and cultural role prescriptions and saw motherhood as central to their identity and purpose.[9] Accepting the prescribed female role, even if only ideologically, has a crucial effect on the course of the woman's career in addiction. In the following paragraphs, I discuss motherhood among women addicts. Beginning with fertility, pregnancy, and birth, I examine motherhood while addicted and the increased inability to take care of the business of mothering, and finally, the realization of narrowing options.

Fertility, Pregnancy, and Birth

It has been argued both medically and experientially that heroin addiction causes amenorrhea.[10] Most women interviewed claimed that during periods of addiction, they ceased to menstruate. This claim is problematic given changes in the quality of heroin and patterns of addiction.

In terms of purity, the quality of heroin has declined. Winick estimates the decline ranges from 87 percent pure heroin in 1920 to 2 percent today.[11] The possible effect of this decline in potency is changes in bodily alternations produced by heroin. Many heroin addicts routinely take other substances in addition to heroin, and although addicted to heroin, they have relatively mild habits. The women's addiction to heroin may, therefore, cause temporary amenorrhea but cannot be relied upon to eliminate menstruation altogether.

The inflated price and relative scarcity of heroin in the San Francisco Bay area over the last three years has had a great impact on the consistency of heroin use among addicts. It is somewhat rare to find an addict—either male or female—who has lengthy runs as a pure heroin addict; instead, the typical addict is constantly cleaning up, becoming readdicted, and cleaning up, often involuntarily, depending on the availability of heroin.[12]

Changes in quality, availability, and addiction patterns effect the woman addict's fertility, but although she may occasionally miss a menstrual period, amenorrhea cannot be counted on as a form of birth control. However, amenorrhea is often assumed, and pregnancy is not detected until other signs are present.

The state of pregnancy transforms the definition of addiction from a so-called "crime without a victim"[13] to one with a very real victim— the unborn fetus. On this issue, there was more consensus among the women interviewed than on any other single aspect of addiction:

They had contempt for women who remained addicted while pregnant. All but two of the women who had had children while in the heroin life claimed that they had cleaned up when they discovered they were pregnant. Those who had not explained that since they believed heroin addiction caused them to stop menstruating and, hence, ovulating, they also believed they could not become pregnant. Many had not discovered that they were pregnant until relatively late (the fourth or fifth month), and by this time, it was both too late to have a simple first-trimester abortion and too late to clean up.

The rationale for continuing heroin use is: (1) if the heroin is going to have an ill effect on the fetus, it has already done so by the fourth or fifth month; and (2) going through withdrawal late in pregnancy is more dangerous than continuing use and giving birth to an addicted baby. This attitude characterized only a few of the women interviewed, who were also able to report numerous incidences where babies were born with a heroin habit, underwent the horrors of withdrawal, and sometimes died. The reliability of the women's accounts about their own drug use during pregnancy is questionable; nevertheless, one ethic remains strong among women in the heroin world: It is not acceptable to remain addicted while pregnant, thereby risking addiction in a newborn baby. This woman's statement represented the predominant view:

> I have a thing about that [being addicted while pregnant]. I won't use drugs while I'm pregnant. It's not fair to the baby. The baby didn't say he wanted to get strung out. And it'll go right to the baby. I really feel strong about that. I only did it [heroin] a few times [maybe once a month] while I was pregnant, but I wouldn't get strung out.

The infant born to an addict is often premature and suffers from the complications of all premature births. Low birth weight is also common among babies of addicts, and withdrawal symptoms are sometimes manifested.[14] A physician described newborn withdrawal:

> Toward the end of the first 24 hours of life, the infant became very restless and irritable, and exhibited marked tremors and twitchings. Blood calcium was examined and found to be normal. Shortly thereafter, vomiting and diarrhea occurred accompanied by constant shrill, high pitched crying and refusal to take feedings. Accompanying these symptoms were persistent nasal stuffiness, increased sweating and a rise in temperature to slightly over 100° F. There were several bouts of intermittent cyanosis within the first 48 hours.[15]

Giving birth while addicted is a horror. The mother often suffers toxemia and other serious complications stemming from poor prenatal care as well as addiction.[16] For the mother who is either currently addicted or has a history of addiction, childbirth can entail psychological battering by hospital staff. Many women complained that even though they were drug-free at the time of birth, the nurses treated them with intense disrespect. (The hospital setting is sometimes the woman addict's first encounter with the social stigma attached to addiction.)

The attitude of hospital staff can set up a pattern of continued failure to comply with medical prescription for proper health care. When pregnant addicts see a physician prior to delivery, they are often treated with disdain because they are addicted. Occasionally, a sympathetic physician will attempt to see them through the pregnancy, sometimes suggesting that they not attempt withdrawal in order to protect the fetus from possible death; it is more likely that the woman will be implored to clean up, lest her baby become addicted. If the woman cannot clean up, she feels that hospital personnel are disgusted with her, hence, she tends to stay away. Therefore, when she comes in contact again with the medical world at the time of delivery, she is treated with disrespect, not only because she is a heroin addict, but because she has failed to follow the standard prenatal routine of seeing a physician regularly.

The combination of psychological battering by the hospital staff and the problems of caring for a withdrawing and ill baby can serve to spiral the woman deeper into addiction. She often feels tremendous guilt over having delivered an addicted baby and generally lacks the support of family or close friends; in short, she feels she has failed at motherhood almost before it has begun.

Mothering While Addicted

The mother who can maintain a heroin habit and take care of her children is respected in the heroin world. Although all women felt that caring for their children was most important, some were better able to accomplish the joint tasks of addiction and mothering than others. The women who were best able to combine heroin and children were those whose childcare responsibilities forced them to control their drug use; in fact, a woman would occasionally indicate that she had become pregnant and had a baby in order to control her use of heroin. But for those women whose children were not born for the purpose of controlling their use and routinizing their lives, it was an accomplishment to discipline themselves, so that their children's needs were met before their own for heroin. Just as successfully combining motherhood and a career is a source of pride to the nondrug-using woman, the ability to combine responsible mothering and heroin use is a source of pride to the addicted mother. As one woman said:

> I have custody of her. The State, you know, the police, filed to take her away from me, and the Health Department said my little girl has hypergammaglobulin anemia and her shots run me $340 a month. She gets a shot a week. And the Welfare Department told the court that she was the healthiest baby they had seen in a long time. I already had her in Head Start, you know, preschool at three years old. She was already starting to read. She could count up to 50 at three. She was clean, she had clothes and food. She was always in bed by 7:30–8:00 P.M. I was always up in the morning cooking breakfast. They said even though I had a narcotic problem and from what people told them too, like days when all I had was enough money to fix, but I would make sure she was taken care of. And if I didn't have enough money to take care of her and fix, she would be taken care of—I wouldn't. I'd go sick.

A few women were able to carve out a routine incorporating their children's needs with their own. These two women put it well:

> I get up in the morning, go and cop—oh, about getting up in the morning—luckily my daughter has adjusted her sleeping hours to mine, so I get up in the morning, get her dressed and fed and all that. And then I proceed to see who's out and who I can cop from. And I cop and I stay out, you know, like if there are any of my regular tricks, I'll stay out and try to make some money. And then I'll go back home. I get home about 5–6–7 P.M., get the baby ready for bed, feed her, fix again, and go out and make as much money as I can; make the rent money, make the food money, and make my money to fix.

The other woman notes:

> Oh, after I fixed, she'd eat, right? That wasn't nothin' but formula and a little cereal 'cause by then it would be 9:30–10:00 A.M. before she'd wake back up. Then she'd be in there [tub] when I'd bathe and she loves water. She'd want to get in there. After I had fed her, then she'd go back to sleep. Then it's time

for me to do mine again. It's sad, but it's true. I go and do my thing again, and by that time, I'd get myself together as far as putting on clothes, taking my shower, washing up, whatever. After that, I'd sit and watch TV and nod.

When an addicted mother was able to establish a routine for her heroin use, she was in an optimal position to raise her children in a manner with which she felt comfortable. For the exceptional mother, combining heroin and children meant controlling her habit and competent care of her children. The woman addict who is at the top of the heroin hierarchy, such as the successful dealer or spouse of a dealer, is best able to handle childcare: She has constant access to heroin, does not have to leave her home to work, and, therefore, can be both well (not withdrawing) and available to her children.

As previously mentioned, the addict hierarchy and stratification system is fluid; the woman at the top may find herself either incarcerated or poor, sick, and hustling in the street in a very short time. Therefore, the mother who at one point can perform her childcare duties by controlling her heroin usage and organizing her life may suddenly find her world in chaos. If she is suffering withdrawal because she hasn't the money to buy drugs or drugs are not available, it is difficult for her to take care of children of any age but especially babies and small children. Thus, older children are often given the responsibility of caring for babies. As one woman related:

I do everything I can to make her stop crying and if she still keeps crying, I just let her cry. I stick her in the other room and close the door and let her cry—turn up the TV and then she'll cry herself to sleep. The three year old, ummm, she's well; they are both excellent kids. I don't know what I did to deserve them. [She shakes her head and shrugs her shoulders.] But they are really very easy to get along with. [She says this with obvious affection.] If I say, "Mama don't feel good today" to the three year old, she'll pretty much leave me alone. She'll occupy her sister, her little sister's time, mama her, give her the bottle, rock her.

It is also likely that the woman in these circumstances will have to resort to illegal street work to support herself (prostitution, boosting, forgery). When the addict-mother has to leave her home in order to work to support her habit or even to buy drugs, she encounters the same difficulties with childcare that other working mothers do. In addition, she is usually making very little money and is often not organized enough to know how and where to look for competent childcare. Consequently, she is sometimes forced to leave small children alone while she goes out to score or hustle; as might be expected, this can result in neglect at best and tragedy at worst.[17]

The use of potent or excessive heroin can also have a deleterious effect on the woman's ability to mother: She may go on the nod and be incapable of responding to the needs of her children. In this condition, she is functionally absent. One woman discussed two of her friends:

> This girl had been using since she was 12. One source said her baby died when she was nodding and he got a hold of some of her Ritalins. He ate them and died in the hospital. I had another friend who had nine kids. Now she doesn't have any of them. One of her kids got killed while she was nodding on the couch. The kid went out in the street and got hit by a car. Turned out to be a vegetable and wound up dying.

Although addicted, the mother with money who works at home, whether as a dealer or housewife, can often control her drug use and perform her childcare tasks (often quite admirably). But the fluid nature of the heroin world can quickly change her situation. She may escape jail but still find her life in a state of chaos that, coupled with withdrawal sickness, leads to child neglect. Street work forces the woman to be away from home and children, and thus makes her unable to care for them. The psychoactive effects of heroin can produce a state of euphoria, so that the woman is not in a position to carry out routine mothering tasks because she is on the nod. The experience of the average woman in the life—that of chaos and inundation—results in a general inability to take care of the business of mothering.

Dealing with the Inability to Take Care of Business

For the woman who recognizes her own inability to parent, who cannot control her heroin use and wants a better home for her children, the move to place her children in another environment is likely to be voluntary. The woman often has family members who are willing to take the children, so they do not have to be placed in foster homes or institutions. I found this to be the case most often among black women, who had mothers, aunts, and sisters who were available. The arrangement was seen as temporary and did not have the impact and guilt that characterizes losing children to institutions. One woman recalled:

When I used to get hooked, everything seemed gray. I didn't
realize what I was doing. . . . nothing around me mattered.
Even my kids didn't matter to me. I brought my kids to my
mother and dropped them off. I'd give her money for them
and all that shit, but I was gone. It was just that fix and that
was it.

Another described what she did while addicted:

. . . she was never neglected. If she was, I would give her to
his mother and tell her, "Hey, I can't handle her right now." I
would never keep her if I couldn't handle her.

When a neighbor or even a landlord who is concerned or upset
about children who seem ill, neglected, or both notifies the child welfare department, a social worker then calls on the family in question
to survey the situation. If the child is not severely injured, guide-
lines are usually set for the parents. A social worker describes the
procedure.

I would get a phone call from neighbors, landlords, sometimes
even relatives, complaining that the child is being neglected.
Sometimes babies are left alone or unchanged. They constantly
smell like urine. Occasionally, the call reports battering, but
that occurs less than just general neglect. I go out to the home,
look around, and try to determine how serious the problem is.
With the junkies, I tell them, "Okay, you get your [welfare]
check on the first and get your food stamps. Before you buy
anything else, I want you to buy two weeks worth of Pampers,
two weeks worth of Similac, and *then*, if you must, the
heroin."

Infrequently, the addicted mother is deemed unfit by the social
agency, and her children are forcibly taken away from her. Welfare
agencies do not want to take children away from their mothers, but if
persistent neglect or harm is evident, they do. If the woman's family
is available and cooperative, the children are placed with them; if not,
they are placed in foster homes or institutions. Forcible or involuntary removal of children is, of course, a more difficult emotional experience for the mother than voluntary removal.

In the areas of motherhood and the fear of losing children, women
addicts differ greatly from addicted men but very closely resemble
other women in the larger society. By looking at a group of women
who appear wholly deviant in occupational, physical, and social

realms, it is possible to understand the pervasive nature of culture; specifically, the prescribed role of the mother in our culture and society and the way in which it is assumed. Our culture and society do make specific claims about the role of mother,[18] and women addicts, who cannot be considered ideologically liberated as defined by the women's movement, tend very much to accept society's prescriptions for this role. They see themselves as primarily responsible for their children (in contrast to the responsibility that they attribute to the children's father, which is generally extremely small). They also feel that motherhood is their single claim to worthiness; it is often their greatest responsibility. Additionally, women addicts subscribe to the notion that motherhood and fulfilling its responsibilities is the core of their own femininity. Failing at this endeavor is, therefore, equivalent, not only to being irresponsible, but to failing at womanhood in general. Because removing an addict-mother's children is socially and emotionally devastating, she attempts to forestall this almost inevitable event if possible. The threat of losing her children becomes the central element of risk in the addict-mother's life.

When children are placed in alternative homes, either voluntarily or involuntarily, the woman often ceases to attempt to control her heroin habit at all. She has given up or lost her children who had provided the impetus for keeping it together. This loss can begin a further spiraling downward into the addiction life with no holds barred. As this woman said:

> My mom called up the welfare department and said she wanted the baby put in a foster home. I got the papers served on me, went to court. They made him a ward of the court and put him in a foster home. He was two years old then. That's when I went downhill all the way. I tried at first, but they wouldn't let me see the baby for two months and I couldn't handle that. . . . nothin' was going right, and I just started using heavy and heavy and heavy.

Realization of Narrowing Options

The woman begins her career in drugs with relatively reduced options: In addition to having female status, she is often poor and of a racial minority; her occupational opportunities are few due to limited educational and job skill training. Therefore, motherhood is often viewed by such women as one of the more desirable options in terms of social worth, and it is one of the only viable roles for them; yet this role is likely to be seen as "given" until it is threatened.

There are several ways that motherhood can be threatened: by physical abuse, prolonged separations, rejection by the child due to disapproval for the mother's lifestyle, or by the child adopting the heroin life. Women who could bring themselves to discuss abusing their children often feared that this abuse would destroy the mother-child relationship. As this woman said:

> My son, when I first came out the penitentiary the first time, he had done something. God knows what it was, but it wasn't anything he had done. It was a little thing that provoked what I was feeling 'cause I couldn't get a fix. And I just beat him unmercifully. Just unmerciful. God, Jesus! He doesn't remember. I've never told him either. That's the one thing I've never told him. But I've never forgotten it either. This one beating with my kid made me make a really fast decision. I sold all my furniture, packed up my clothing, and went to my grandmother's. Never once again did I try to take the responsibility of him while addicted or drinking. I don't give a damn what anybody says, I've seen it tried a thousand and one times. Addicts cannot have their children with them. I don't give a damn how together they think they are, their kids suffer. Believe me. And their loved ones suffer. Everybody suffers around them. It isn't intended to be that way, but that's the way it is. And pretty soon, those feelings are just ice cold. All you think about is that damned monkey on your back. And everything goes. No matter how they say they got it together. And I'm speaking from my own experience plus my experience I have experienced with other people while I was hooked. And I know that you cannot be addicted and be a good mother. If you are addicted, just leave. Get away from them 'cause you are going to hurt them first.

Sometimes mistreatment takes the form of housing children in a negative environment as much as physical neglect. As this woman described:

> It was just too much for me, the whole thing. My house was starting to turn into a shooting gallery. People would come over, "Let me get down here, let me get down here." I only had the one little girl at the time, but she was really mimicking, you know? She'd pick up a piece of straw and pretend like it was an outfit and it just blew me away when I saw her do that and so I said, "I'm cleaning up."

Women who have been active in the heroin life and have been separated from their children feel guilty about their absence:

> When my son was born and he was just a few months old is
> when I started getting into it again, and I was spending as little
> time as I could with them. If they weren't with my mother, one
> of my friends were taking care of them, and I just was always
> tripping somewhere. I mean, I'd be gone two or three days,
> and they'd be with the kids. I always had the kids taken care
> of well. I mean, I never neglected them or anything like that
> but, you know, I do look back and have guilt feelings about the
> way I just shoved my kids off.

Some women feel that the separation deprived their children of some
of the advantages they could have provided:

> I feel that if I didn't get strung out, they would have had their
> home, they probably would have gone to parochial school,
> they would have had so much more. They probably would
> have been in Girl Scouts and Boy Scouts, and they would have
> had a different home life. But instead, they had to get shifted
> to their grandparents' house; mommy was in jail, mommy was
> a dope fiend. I always had everything I wanted, so I feel, like
> in my subconscious mind, I just give my kids whatever they
> want because, I guess I feel bad because I deprived them of
> some things, which is no good. I'm not doing them any good
> by doing what I'm doing.

Women who have spent a good deal of time incarcerated also have a
sense that they have missed important developmental stages in their
children's lives:

> I missed so much out of my daughter's childhood when she
> was growing that I wanted to have another baby because of
> things I missed. Like, I never saw her when she rode her bike
> for the first time—stupid things like that, which a lot of people
> wouldn't understand. Like, she lost her front teeth and grew
> 'em back before I got out of the penitentiary.

Possibly the most frightening part of realizing that role options are
narrowing in regard to mothering is a child's maturation. Since one of
the central aspects of mothering seems to be providing a role model,
many women feared that when their children matured and became
cognizant of their mother's drug use, they would reject her. Neglect
of basic childcare, some mistreatment, and even separation could be

remedied, but setting a negative example when the children were old enough to understand was not acceptable. Some women fear and wonder how they will look to the child. As this woman said:

> He doesn't know. He knows that sometimes I'm very irritable and edgy. He knows that sometimes I sleep a lot from being sick or from staying up all night using. He's gotten pretty independent from it actually. I don't feel good about it, because a lot of times when I'm sick, I can't really be there for him in the way that I'd like. Or I read to him when I'm loaded and he thinks I'm tired. I'm sure he can pick up certain vibes—I'm more there in certain ways when I'm clean than when I'm not, but he doesn't know the details. He knows we smoke weed. He's six and a half. That it's a positive drug, it's part of my value system. He knows it's illegal, and we don't talk about it but that we do it. Same with sex. But I don't share the dope thing. I don't feel bad keeping it from him. I'd feel a whole lot worse sharing it with him because there's no way he can relate to it now. Since I see it as part of my life off and on forever, I don't know whether I'm going to go on keeping it from him or someday when he's a teenager he'll put it together. It kind of freaks me because I can't accept it in myself, and I want to be a model for him.

Other women fear that their children will accept them as role models and become addicts themselves. No woman interviewed wanted her child or anyone she cared for to become addicted. As one woman put it:

> The only reason why I really want to quit and the one that gives me power to quit is for the baby. Or else, I wouldn't even try it. I'd just keep going like nothin'. Shit, what the hell? Now that I have the baby, I have something to think about, 'cause when he gets older and he knows what I'm doing, I don't want him to—I don't even want him to see me do that 'cause I don't want my kid to turn out like me, no way. I'd really regret that. I'd really feel bad about that.

Conclusion

The male addict prides himself on taking care of business when he organizes his life around his heroin habit and is able to maintain himself in this routine.[19] Heroin becomes the focus of his life and takes precedence over all other endeavors. For the woman with children, however, taking care of heroin-related business cannot be her central concern. Therefore, although men and women fare similarly in the early stages of addiction, women with children have a decided disadvantage in later maintenance phases.

When the woman addict senses that she is in a position to lose her children, either psychologically or physically, she begins to take serious stock of her situation. Since motherhood is central to her feminine identity, the label of "unfit" and subsequent loss of children is tantamount to the loss of her womanhood; she often feels intense guilt and a sense of failure over this loss. In many ways, losing her children represents a greater risk than incarceration or the other threatening aspects of the heroin life. At this point in the woman's career, she realizes that her motherhood options are, indeed, being funneled and that the sacrifice she makes for heroin is getting closer to her own person, identity, and sense of self. One woman pointed out:

> When you realize that you are losing your kids, your womanhood, to that monkey on your back, that's when you've gotta get out.

The realization of narrowing options provides the impetus for the attempt out of the heroin life. Knowing that she has already put her occupational options in jeopardy, the woman can gear herself toward abstinence from heroin in order to protect the remaining option of a viable family life.[20] While she still has something to lose, the one option of motherhood, she is in an optimal frame of mind for getting out of the heroin life, ending her career in addiction.

CHAPTER SEVEN

Getting the Treatment

The expansion of drug treatment facilities has been so great that when an addict makes a commitment to cleaning up and getting out of the heroin life, s/he most often thinks in terms of treatment as an aid, sometimes a salvation; this chapter is devoted to a discussion of the treatment process. I look at the treatment scene and modes of treatment, including detoxification and methadone maintenance, as well as the structural problems encountered by women desiring treatment and their difficulties in treatment: credibility, physiological problems, therapy, and sexism. The disillusionment experienced by women who have attempted treatment and the ways in which they subsequently treat themselves and use the facilities are examined. In addition, I discuss the deleterious aspects of treatment and how repeated recidivism stemming from the treatment's structure serves to lock women into the heroin life by actualizing the "once a junkie, always a junkie" prophecy.

The Treatment Scene

Over the last decade the treatment scene, as it is called in the heroin world, has grown fantastically; millions of dollars in federal, state, and private monies have been used to set up a variety of treatment programs and projects. The assumption behind establishing these facilities is that such programs help users to clean up for the purpose of becoming permanently opiate-free; much research indicates, however, that this goal is not being met.[1] While it is indeed true that one must clean up in order to get out of the heroin world, treatment in no way ensures that an addict will abstain from heroin or even clean up temporarily. Treatment has become part of the heroin world, part of the heroin life, and a drug phenomenon of its own.

A Bridge

The treatment scene has become part of the heroin world by functioning as a bridge between addict and nonaddict lifestyles. Programs introduce the drug culture into a supposedly drug-free environment; for the addict, being in treatment as a patient eases the culture shock of total separation from the heroin world. If the staff people are ex-addicts, there is even more commonality among staff and patients. As one woman noted:

> There was one good aspect that I liked about treatment—all the counselors were ex-drug users and . . . you don't catch that attitude. It was very low key. They were talking about peer group. I found that more comfortable than any other kind.

Being a staff person in a treatment facility can be the perfect compromise for the ex-addict. Such a situation is analogous to that of the poverty programs in the 1960's, as Tom Wolfe describes:

> Everybody but the most hopeless lames knew that the only job you wanted out of the poverty program was a job in the program itself. Get on the payroll, that was the idea. Never mind getting some job counseling. You be the job counselor. You be the "neighborhood organizer." As a job counselor or a neighborhood organizer, you stood to make six or seven hundred dollars a month and you were still your own man. That was a very flexible arrangement. You were still on the street and you got paid for it. You could still run with the same buddies you always ran with. There was nobody looking over your shoulder. You didn't have to act like a convert, like the wino who has to sing hymns at the mission before he can get his dinner, to get something out of the poverty scene. In fact, the more outrageous you were, the better. That was the only way they knew you were a real leader. It was true that middle-class people who happened to live in the target areas got the top jobs, but there was still room for street types.[2]

Jobs for ex-addicts as counselors have remained in the face of a widescale evaporation of federal funding. As Winick notes:

> Some observers have pointed to the irony that the "new careers for the poor" movement of the 1960s has largely collapsed. . . . The "new career" that has enjoyed the largest ex-

pansion is in the treatment of opiate users, as staff members of
therapeutic communities, research assistants in methadone
maintenance programs, and the like.[3]

Modalities

There are two basic kinds of treatment available to the addict today: detoxification and methadone maintenance. In the following
paragraphs, I look at the specific kinds of treatment within the broad
category of detoxification and then turn to a history and description
of methadone maintenance.

Detoxification. Drug detoxification facilities have been in operation
for several decades. The original programs were in hospitals, such as
Lexington in Kentucky, which opened in 1935, where addicts went to
be "detoxed." These facilities are still in use, and addicts are often detoxed with methadone.

The therapeutic community was an innovation in drug treatment
during the 1950's; the participating addict became a resident in an
opiate-free community (such as Synanon). The basic ideology was
that addicts must be physically separated from the heroin world and
resocialized before they could embark on a life of total abstinence.[4]

Over the last ten years, a new drug treatment program has been
proliferated—the free clinic. In these quasi-medical facilities, addicts
receive "kicking pills" in a routinized fashion and are given counseling as well. There are often waiting lists to get into such programs,
which are governed by strict rules about the amount of drugs the addict can receive. The Haight-Ashbury Clinic is an example of the free-
clinic treatment modality. Located in an old Victorian house in the
Haight-Ashbury district of San Francisco, the Haight Clinic is painted
in bright colors of the counterculture style of the 1960's and sparsely
furnished with used furniture. Although it is a medical facility in the
sense that prescriptions are dispensed, it appears from the outside
and the lobby to be anything but a traditional medical institution. The
staff at the Haight Clinic dresses casually in a style consistent with
the neighborhood and the clientele—jeans, open shirts, and casual
shoes (not a white coat to be found there). In short, it is very difficult
to tell the clients from the staff from the neighborhood dwellers.

The addict who comes to the clinic is first interviewed about her/
his problem and what s/he wants out of the program. A urinalysis
then determines if s/he is, indeed, an addict. The prescription will
depend on the size of the heroin habit and general drug-using pat-

terns. The addict is routinely given both pills to ease withdrawal and psychological counseling. The enrollee comes to the clinic every day for 21 days to pick up pills and has weekend, take-home privileges. (There is a certain nervousness on Fridays around the clinic.) After 21 days, the addict is dropped from the program and cannot enroll again for at least one month.

Methadone Maintenance. Methadone was developed during World War II in Germany; it was called "Dolophine" and used as a substitute for morphine. It was first used in this country in 1948 on a detox basis—that is, addicts were given methadone on a temporary basis to overcome heroin withdrawal symptoms. Several characteristics of methadone made it an attractive long-term treatment modality: It was inexpensive to manufacture and distribute, and because it was administered every 24 hours, patients had to report to the clinic daily. Most important, however, the addict did not have to resort to illegal means to support her/his drug habit—the drug was supplied free or for a nominal sum. Best of all, the addict could lead a normal, productive life because s/he would not be strung out on heroin, nor would s/he experience a physical craving for the drug.[5] Thus, on two fronts methadone provided an attractive mode of treatment: It alleviated the drug-related crime problem by distributing the drug for a nominal fee (to the patient or the state) and mandatory reporting to the clinic on a daily basis ensured that addicts were available for other forms of therapy such as psychological counseling. Society would be better off and so would the addict.

Although the long-term effects of methadone were not known (as with many other drugs), methadone maintenance programs were opened in 1963. By 1968, there were 1000 users, and five years later in 1973, the number of addicts maintained on methadone had jumped to 86,000.[6]

There are two different long-range goals for the methadone patient and a variety of daily routines that vary with each treatment program and clinic. Some proponents of methadone maintenance see it as a six to nine-month detoxification where the addict starts with a dosage high enough to sate the craving for heroin and cut withdrawal symptoms. The dosage is then gradually lowered until s/he is opiate-free. In another methadone plan, the addict remains on methadone indefinitely at a stabilized dose. The daily routines also differ from program to program, but basically is as follows: The patient must report to the clinic daily, usually early in the morning or around noon; in order to get the methadone, the patient must produce a urine specimen. (In the early programs, there was another requirement for women: In order to enroll in the program, they had to be with a man. The idea was to attract men to the program.) After the urine is collected, the patient is given the methadone, which is drunk in the presence of the clinic staff person. Periodically, urine samples are tested for opiate or barbiturate content, and with enough violations, the patient can be dismissed from the program. (It is rather ironic, as Fort notes, that a person can be dismissed for doing what s/he came to the program to be treated for.)[7] Once the methadone has been taken, the addict is free to leave for the day. (Some patients have take-home privileges.)

Problems

Women addicts experienced several problems with regard to treatment and the treatment scene. First, there were the structural problems of limited space and inadequate facilities; next, there was a credibility gap: The women found it difficult to subscribe to an opiate-free lifestyle when they observed that the people advocating this lifestyle were not drug-free themselves. Then, the physiological problems encountered by women, especially those on methadone, made treatment a difficult endeavor; finally, the problem of therapy and sexism in treatment was sufficient to disillusion many women.

The Structure

When an addict decides to clean up and is truly committed to abstinence, it is imperative to start treatment immediately. Treatment programs often defeat their own purpose by closing the door. As one woman said:

> They should make it real easy for people to clean up. They should make it real easy, because sometimes you can make a decision in your head, "Okay, I don't want to do drugs anymore. I want to clean up." It should be the easiest thing in the world to go somewhere and get whatever you can get that's not addictive to help you kick.

Another woman said:

> I'd like to see more programs for people who are addicted. . . . I was talking to my connection downtown, and there is nowhere she can go to get detoxed even if it were a serious

attempt at changing her whole life. She's been to a couple of places and can't go back.

The decision to clean up is often spontaneous, and it is extremely difficult to predict either success or failure at abstinence. Since many (if not most) addicts need some form of medication to help them through the difficulty of withdrawal, it is important for treatment facilities to remain readily available to both addicts who have not used treatment in the past and to those who have failed in prior attempts at abstinence.

Women addicts, unlike men, very often have family obligations that are constant. If a treatment program cannot (or will not) take into account a woman's family, it is very often unacceptable to her. For example, a married woman whose husband is also addicted said:

> We always go together. We wait for shots together. A couple of times it ended up costing us more money, a lot of money, just having to wait an extra week or two for both of us to get into treatment.

The single most important obstacle faced by women going into treatment—either in-house or out-patient—is the lack of facilities for children,[8] which is especially true of in-house detox programs. As one mother explained:

> I never really could go all the way through the halfway house because I had kids and without my kids, I'd be—good God, I don't know where I'd be. I'd probably be dead from an overdose, because my kids are the ones that keep me down. These halfway houses want you to go for a year or something like that. But I've got kids. I can't go anywhere for a year.

As noted earlier, women's major motivating force for ceasing heroin use is concern for their children and their role as mothers. If going to treatment forces women to further neglect their children, it is counter-productive. While women are motivated to clean up *because* of their children, they will often not go to treatment if facilities are not available *for* children.

Credibility

"I didn't think too much of treatment because my counselor was hooked."

Employing ex-addicts as counselors has produced a good amount of resentment by the addicts whom they counsel. Many women complained that treatment programs are hypocritical because while claiming to *treat* addiction, many of the employees themselves use drugs.[9] As one woman put it:

> I could never handle it [treatment] because I thought it was a big, phony deal. I know a lot of people who have been through it, and I was even thinking that maybe it was the answer for me. But then I'd see them the next day on the corner waiting to cop. No, to me that's hypocritical, very hypocritical. If there's anything I don't like, it's a bunch of ex-addicts, and they are all damned well using too! They are telling you, "What are you using for, you dirty bitch?" I don't like that. Who are you to tell me when you are doing it too? And you can't say that to them in them [treatment] houses because you'll get them in trouble and have them lose their job or whatever. So, you kind of have to sit there and be hypocritical.

Another woman complained:

> We tried a detox program one time, and we ran into two people who were buying dope from us regularly while we were trying to kick. They were making their money by working in the detox clinic.

Another aspect of treatment that seems hypocritical to some women is the financial one. As one woman put it, the sincerity of the staff is questionable, since funding for programs depends on the number of people in treatment:

> They want proof on paper that they straightened you out. They just love it when you are straightening out. When you ain't, they just hate it. And they aren't exactly that nice. But they just love it when you get your shit together and are cleaning up. Then they write down on their records this one cleaned up, and I guess they get a little extra dough for it.

Another woman said:

> Most of them [treatment programs] aren't any good. Like if I'm going to do anything about my habit, I'll do it myself, because they're just there to make money. They're not really there to help you.

Physiological Problems

Interaction between the counselor who determines what drugs and dosage are to be given out and the addict resembles bartering. In such detoxification treatment as the free clinics, the addict often wants a higher dosage or a certain kind of drug to help alleviate withdrawal; the counselor, who typically suspects the addict's motives, wants to keep the dosage low and the drug relatively mild. If the dosage is not high enough to help the woman addict cope with withdrawal symptoms, she may feel that she cannot get through kicking and, instead, turn to heroin to alleviate her symptoms.

Physiological problems from methadone that affect all addicts are much more intense and have a greater impact on their lives; these problems include constipation, sweating, anorexia, nausea, and fluid retention.[10] Methadone can be successful in blocking the addict's craving for heroin and in alleviating heroin withdrawal symptoms. The success depends on the dosage given: At extremely high dosages (100 mg. plus), a user cannot get high on heroin; as the dosage is lowered, however, there is still no physical craving, but it is possible to feel the euphoric effects of other drugs, including heroin. It must be noted, however, that at the same high dosage that totally blocks the addict's ability to experience a heroin high, there are a number of side effects—the most conspicuous is that the methadone user goes to sleep spontaneously. Since spontaneous sleep makes a normal lifestyle difficult, the methadone treatment falls short of its goals. Two different women illustrated this point; the first spoke about her mother, who was on methadone:

> They started her off on something like 100 mg. . . . she was trying to hold a job and do that at the same time. She ended up getting fired really quick because she slept all day at her job.

The other woman described her own experience:

> When I first got on methadone, they didn't know how much to give a person, and I was at 120 mg., which was very, very high. . . . I'd be cooking dinner and I'd nod out at the stove. My hair would catch fire. I was just bombed all the time.

Spontaneous sleep could easily result in a fire since a disproportionate number of addicts are smokers. Driving poses another problem:

Behind methadone, I've burned holes in the mattress this big. God, I woke up and the whole room was smelling. . . . I burned more clothes, it was ridiculous. I would go visit people, and they would swear I was still using because I could not keep my eyes open. Driving, I would have to have the radio on full blast and the windows down or I'd be driving and trying to keep my head up.

Aside from spontaneous sleep, there are several other immediate side effects from using methadone: perspiration, constipation, lethargy, short-term memory lapse, heart problems, sexual problems, extreme withdrawal symptoms, fetal addiction and infant withdrawal, water retention, and weight gain. One woman described some of her problems with perspiration and inertia:

When I got on methadone, I didn't have the incentive to do the things I did before, like I'm interested in painting and art. I found myself just sitting around and wanting to read all the time. I've always been a reader, but I find myself doing this abnormally. I'm just physically and mentally lazy. Plus, it also causes you to perspire a lot. Just the slightest physical exertion, just sweeping the floor, and tons of perspiration pouring off my body. Oh, it's terrible. You know, when you go anywhere and you try to put on make-up, it's running all off.

Another woman talked about her heart problems:

Methadone crystallizes and when it crystallizes, it usually crystallizes in your joints. When people are coming down from methadone, their joints ache. It's worse than stuff because it saturates, whereas heroin goes right through your blood. This [methadone] saturates and stays. It's like strychnine. It builds and builds. Okay, it crystallized in my left ventricle, and it stopped the normal amount of blood and oxygen into the heart. They had to actually flush the ventricle. I was in the hospital for seven weeks.

Another woman related the sexual problems her husband was having:

For the most part, he just isn't able to perform sexually on methadone. It's much worse than the heroin. It not only takes the desire away, physically he's just not able to do it.

These are just a few of the known, immediate side effects from methadone; there is no way of knowing what the result of using methadone daily for 10, 15, or 20 years will be. The effect of using heroin for long periods seems to be rather benign. Heroin addiction also tends to come in runs lasting weeks, months, or years, with breaks in between due to prison or voluntary abstinence. Such is not the case with methadone maintenance, however, which might involve a lifetime run.

Therapy and Sexism

Therapy is often a requirement in treatment programs. It may take the form of one-on-one or "grouping," and it may involve humiliating the patient (Synanon style). In order to remain in the treatment program (and not be sent back to prison), women forced to participate in therapy often play the game. As one woman related:

> I hated the things they make you do when you come in there. God, they make you stand up on a chair and scream, "I need help," until they thought I was screaming loud enough so they thought they were getting some feeling from me. They kept saying they didn't feel it. I said to myself, "I guess not." Standing up there on that stupid chair, I felt like hollering, "I don't need your help!" But I knew if I messed up, I'd get sent back to court and jail, so I stood up there and hollered my head off.

Much of the "gaming" is aimed at the psychological dissipation of each participant. The goal is to strike at the core of the individual's identity in order to rebuild; for women, the source of humiliation is often their failure at motherhood. Hempden-Turner writes about two women who were dissipated at the Delancy Street Foundation. The subject of one Chicana's dissipation was her son, who had committed murder, rape, and sodomy. The participants in the game directly attributed his transgressions to her addiction and failure at motherhood. The second woman was blamed for the deaths of her two children—the first, who drowned in the bath while she fixed and lost consciousness; and the second, who was born deformed and died immediately. In both instances, the woman's identity, unlike that of the men who were targets, hinged on their roles as mothers.[11]

Women become "psychologized" after participating in treatment: Before the women in this study had revealed the nature of their treatment experience to the interviewers, it was clear that they had been in some kind of therapy by their use of terminology, elaborate self-analysis, the belief in personality inadequacy as the root of their addiction. Often psychological labeling backfires:

> It [therapy] made me feel really bad about myself, and I didn't feel like getting myself together. I felt like I really couldn't make it in the straight world even though I'd gotten clean (for three whole weeks I was clean) it was just a joke to her [counselor]. It was a setback to me because it was hard for me to ask for help. It seemed so strange to me that she said I had an addictive personality because everybody has an addictive personality whether they're addicted to religion or their job or their morning coffee or whatever. People are very compulsive about it and wrap their whole lives around it, and I thought it was really bizarre that she was saying that to *me*. It made me feel real dependent, too, because I felt that she was saying that I was weak, and if I wasn't addicted to heroin, I would be addicted to alcohol or my old man or my over-protective mother—that I had some deficiency that made me a clinger. I think being a woman, I feel some of that anyway—that I'm not as strong and independent as I would like to be.

Many women in this study indicated that hypocrisy was what they felt was inherently wrong with treatment. Because the women believed that the treatment milieu was inherently hypocritical due to counselor drug use, the financial aspect, and therapy techniques, it was very difficult for them to commit themselves to the values of the treatment program, and they attached little significance to their own motivations for going to treatment.[12] If treatment was a game to the proponents, then it would be a game for the women too.

A number of researchers have found the treatment milieu to be less than adequate for women on many levels: job skill preparation, psycho-social growth, resocialization, ability to function in the community without drugs.[13] Other researchers have claimed, however, that the *psychological* profile of the woman addict before treatment makes her an unlikely candidate for successful abstinence, regardless of treatment milieu.[14] In attempting to assess objectively the woman addict's motives, self-esteem, level of pathology, and countless other subjective aspects, the researchers have failed to seek subjective *accounts* by women themselves of their failure in treatment. Some noteworthy exceptions to this pattern are Soler, Levy and Doyle, and White, who have found that male-orientation and inherent sexism in treatment make it unsuitable for the woman addict.[15] Therefore, rather than failing in treatment programs, as some researchers have chosen to label the phenomena, I maintain that women are successful in the way they use treatment. Believing that treatment facilities have no real commitment to helping addicts, particularly *women* addicts, they play along—not seeing themselves as failures at all if they recidivate, but seeing, instead, the whole treatment milieu as inherently hypocritical, exploitative, and thus, another facility in the heroin world to be used, in turn, to the addict's advantage.

Disillusionment

The structural, credibility, physiological, and therapeutic problems of treatment often cause the woman addict to become disillusioned with the pretense of the process. This is particularly true when the woman finds that the methadone routine itself creates obstacles to leading a normal, productive life.

In addition to the inherent problem of spontaneous sleep, requiring a urine sample in order to get the methadone dose may be a problem: One has only to imagine a morning routine that postpones urination for an hour or so after rising. Also, the mandatory therapy required in some methadone programs makes holding down a job with specified, required hours impossible. In Reichart and Klein's film *An American Way of Dealing*, Peter Bourne, one of methadone's original proponents, notes that a positive aspect of the methadone program is its ability to control the lives of addicts by requiring them to report to the clinic every day, and he comments on how beneficial this kind of control would prove.[16] Indeed, by forcing daily appearance, other kinds of therapy such as psychological counseling could be used. Addicts, too, feel this control and, not surprisingly, are not so positive about it. Three women commented:

> The stipulation of my parole was that I had to get on methadone or I could not be paroled. But, I can't get on methadone unless I can pee dirty for them, unless I can give them a dirty test full of heroin. So, then you go out and get yourself half-assed hooked so you can get on methadone.

> They have done that to me three times. And in the PDR it says a good dose to maintain anybody is 60 mg. I've always been up on 90. You know, 5 mg. when you're clean will make you nod. . . . I come out of the joint and within 90 days, they got me on 90 mg. The only time I would wake up was to drink my meth-

adone. I was zonked out of my gourd. I was like that for two
years because if you start dropping your milligrams, they can
violate your parole. If you are trying to get off the program,
they'll violate you.

Another woman said:

Methadone scares me. It's a government plot to control people.
Once they hook you on it, they never let you go. You can't
leave town. They've got records. I'd rather have a $200-a-day
habit than go on methadone.

And finally:

I find it rather frightening to have the government have control
of my body that way. I mean, I've thought of a national crisis
or something, like an earthquake for instance. The people on
methadone would be the last people they would care about.
You know, you'd be going for treatment and the methadone
clinic isn't there. There'd be tens of thousands of people that
are seriously injured, and you are going in because you are
dreadfully sick because you are not getting your methadone.
And you know the doctors aren't going to care. You are going
to be the last people that they're going to care about. A bunch
of junkies, as far as they're concerned. I just find the thought
of that, even though it's a remote possibility, really frightening.
And, of course, you lack the personal freedom as far as being
able to take off and go places too.

While methadone was intended to permit addicts to lead normal,
productive lives, spontaneous sleep and the daily routine of procur-
ing methadone make this difficult. It is quite possible, in fact, that
rather than being productive in society, addicts end up costing the
government a great deal of money. All of the women interviewed
who were on methadone were also getting some kind of government
support; none worked at a legitimate paying job.

The situation of women on methadone parallels that of men in the
area of work. For example, based on the criteria of being employed,
off welfare, and uninvolved in criminal or illegal activities, Preble
found that only 20 percent of his respondents could be considered
methadone successes.[17] The results of an extensive evaluation of
methadone maintenance make similar assertions. This research team
says:

the results of methadone maintenance programs as reported in the literature have shown methadone to be a highly effective method of achieving the social rehabilitation of narcotic addicts. This conclusion typically is based upon improvement in employment status and a decrease in both drug abuse and criminality among the patients.

the present data do not appear to be wholly supportive of such a positive evaluation of methadone modalities. The dropout rates, rates of unemployment, and levels of self-reported drug abuse among the methadone patients are somewhat higher than those reported in the literature . . .[18]

Finally, Burt et al. found that success of treatment was independent of any particular treatment modality, including methadone.[19]

Although blocking the physical craving for heroin (and producing, in some addicts, spontaneous sleep), a moderate dosage of methadone will not prevent a user from also getting high on heroin. Consequently, many addicts get on methadone, as with other treatment programs, not because they are committed to cleaning up, but because their routine with heroin is temporarily difficult or impossible to maintain. For example, the connection may have been arrested, cutting off supply for a time; the addict may be without funds; or the addict may be hot with the police. In such cases or similar situations, an addict may use methadone to tide her/him over or to reduce the heroin habit so it is less expensive. Thus, the addict is very often using both methadone and heroin. As one woman noted:

I was using [heroin] all the time after I got on methadone. I never really did stop using [heroin]. But, like I say, I didn't have the kind of habit where I had to make all that money.

And another:

Methadone stops you from having to steal so much, and, you know, you ain't gonna be sick from shit, so everybody I know that's on methadone is sellin' it for dope.

When assessing methadone's success in helping to alleviate the drug-related crime problem, it is necessary to be skeptical.[20] Not only can addicts enjoy heroin along with a moderate dose of methadone, but methadone maintenance may be counter-productive insofar as crime is concerned, because, as Reichart and Klein show, the methadone clinic itself is a place where addicts meet regularly. Although the methadone routine is directed toward helping addicts lead normal, productive lives in which they hold down jobs in the straight world, this is rarely the case. (As already noted, the women interviewed on methadone were also unemployed.) Rather than leaving the methadone clinic immediately after receiving the day's dose and going to work, many methadone addicts hang around for a good part of the day with the result that methadone clinics have become institutionalized places for dealing drugs. As one woman stated:

> Methadone programs are meeting places for people who are dealing dope. People do get their methadone and they shoot dope anyway. They want dope, but they can't have dope, and they still can't quit using it. I don't know if it has helped the crime rate any. People still get loaded. One of the guys that used to drive me around when we'd go stealing was on the methadone maintenance program.

In addition, while the methadone addict on a moderate dose can get high on heroin, it takes more heroin to produce a high; thus, the addict has to score twice as much heroin as before and usually has to resort to illegal means to do so.

Disillusioned with the system, many women drop out of detox treatment and either drop out or violate the rules of methadone maintenance programs. They often resort to self-treatment and use treatment facilities for purposes other than those intended: a means of avoiding prison, controlling their habit, and of engaging in poly-drug use.

Self-Treatment

The most common form of self-treatment through medication is "hitting the doctor." My data indicate that in most cases the woman initiates the visit, knows what kind of medication she wants, and does not let the physician know that she is an addict. There are a variety of "scripts" (prescriptions) used for easing the pain of withdrawal: Valium, codeine, sleeping pills (often called "kicking" pills).

In order to obtain a prescription for kicking drugs, some women interviewed manufactured elaborate stories about bad backs, insomnia, arthritis. Some went to doctors with a reputation on the street for cooperating with such requests; others went to "virgin" doctors whose prescription writing policies were not known. The women were surprisingly successful at getting what they wanted or, at least, getting some kind of medication. As one young addict related:

> People with arthritis have an easy time. If you say you have

arthritis, they'll give you anything. There's no test they can give you to find out if you have arthritis.

Generally, doctors have reputations—the ones that are easy to get dope from. So, you go to the doctor with the reputation. But, sometimes it's better to go to an unknown doctor, one that handles older people, one that wouldn't be so suspicious and worried about you hitting on him for drugs. It's up to the person [the addict], whatever they are good at. I know one girl who is particularly good at it. You know, her arms are fucked up, but she'll wear a blouse that's kind of open in front so he'll [the doctor] look at the tits and not the arms and not notice she's a junkie.

It has been argued that medical and psychiatric practitioners *view* women as basically more psychologically pathological than men.[21] Consequently, women as a class of patients tend to be *treated* as having more psychological problems than men; their medical complaints are diagnosed as psychogenic rather than organic. Hence, women are prescribed psychotropic drugs more frequently than men in both psychiatric and nonpsychiatric settings.[22] It is not at all clear that the psychotropic drugs are being prescribed for actual problems or neurosis or psychosis; instead, an expression of (minor) emotional distress or, very often, a difficult-to-diagnose organic problem will be treated with psychotropic drugs.[23]

Women heroin addicts, many of whom in the past became addicted through legitimate medical prescription,[24] now *use* the physician's perspective to their advantage. They get prescriptions for sedatives when they desire to kick or cool down a heroin habit and sometimes purely for recreational or financial purposes—using drugs (for example, Quaaludes) to get high or sell on the street for a profit. As in many other areas of the heroin world, women addicts utilize sex-role stereotyping and their stigmatized position to their advantage.

If a physician's prescription is not readily available, several kinds of kicking drugs can be procured within the heroin world: barbiturates, Valiums, codeines, Darvons, Ritalin. Alcohol (especially tequila) is used by women to tide them over withdrawal. Another very common form of self-medication is illegal methadone, which can be purchased on the street. Since hitting the doctor is expensive and necessarily short-term, many women have rather elaborate methods of enduring withdrawal by using only street drugs.

Using the Facilities

There has been a newly formed partnership between criminal justice institutions and the drug treatment world: Very often a judge will sentence an addict—male or female—to a treatment program in lieu of prison. As one woman recalled:

> When I went to the program, it [kicking] didn't bother me. Shit, they give you all them crazy pills, and I had just made up my mind that I was going to kick because, at that time, I had a boosting [theft] case, and they wanted to send me to the penitentiary for that. I was lucky enough to get in the program.

For older women or men who have been in the heroin world for many years (for example, 20 plus), treatment can be a last resort, the only potentially viable place left to go. A case in point is "Sue," who is 48, serving a sentence in city prison, and convinced that treatment is her only hope of piecing together her life, doing something meaningful, and staying out of jail.

> Another good part of my life has been Walden House—helping other people, getting my head together, and working for the first time in years—working to get people out of jail and watching them grow. Goddamn, I loved it and that's what I keep hanging on to. Everybody said, "Oh, man, I'm sorry you have to go to Walden House." I'm not sorry. It's my choice. . . . I know it works and I know that I got a lot of work to do on me.

Treatment is also used by the woman addict to control her habit; there are three major reasons for attempting to do so: (1) the addict is hot with the police, and it is necessary to stop hustling at least temporarily and get off the street; (2) the addict wants to reduce the size of her habit, so that she can get high using less heroin; and (3) she wants to lessen the general hassle of heroin. As Waldorf notes, talking primarily about male addicts:

> Whenever an addict's tolerance develops to such an extent that he finds it difficult to get high or even maintain himself without suffering recurrent or prolonged withdrawal sickness, he will attempt some withdrawal. This is often done on the streets by the addict himself, with the aid of Dolophines, barbiturates, or tranquilizers. With a supply of dollies, the addict can gradu-

ally reduce his tolerance for heroin to a manageable dosage, one that he can afford and that will allow him to get high.

When a detoxification facility is available and he can get into it within a reasonable time, he will use it. The need to reduce tolerances and to ease various pressures from society—to clean up for a court appearance after an arrest, to appease a parole or probation officer's demands to clean up, to obviate pressures exerted by his family—are the principal reasons why addicts go to detoxification facilities. It is very seldom that an addict goes to detoxification because he wants to give up the use of heroin.[25]

Several addicts in the sample reported that they used treatment only to control a habit. Alksne et al. call this form of treatment "maintenance detoxification" and argue that it is one avenue out of heroin addiction.[26] One woman interviewed has been to the Haight-Ashbury Detox Clinic so many times that she is not allowed to come back; she was told that a detox clinic was not a maintenance center. She admitted that she was not using the medication to detoxify:

I'd take the pills and do dope to get my habit down—to taper off so I didn't have to do so much. They can't really help anybody to clean up if they've been shooting righteous dope.

Hospitals are often used in the same way:

I went out to the hospital for seven days, for methadone detox. The day I got out, I shot me some dope. I was clean. I was able to *feel* the dope when I got out.

Another woman, an addict for 18 years, said:

My habit is constant. Maybe five days out of every two years I'd go in the hospital and kick—not kick, but just bring my habit down.

As Carlson describes, avoiding hassle is a primary motivation for going to treatment:

The addict's reasons for going to treatment are always for the resolution of hassle but for some individuals, this hassle is seen as so severe that further heroin use is no longer possible for them. These are the individuals who do stay clean after treatment and who are counted as treatment "successes." For such individuals, treatment provides a way out of a situation which has become intolerable. . . . Other addicts feel that the major portion of their hassle can be relieved by treatment and then they can return to heroin use at a level which is adaptive. These addicts are perceiving heroin as being potentially separate from the hassle.[27]

Addicts very often use the drugs obtained from treatment facilities as recreational drugs to have on hand as an emergency supply:

> B. and I had been coming to the clinic for pills to try to clean up, but all we did was come here and get pills in the morning and save them or take them if we were sick. And then we'd go home and get loaded [on heroin]. . . . Almost everybody that went there didn't really have the intention of cleaning up. They came there just mostly to get the pills when they couldn't score or just to have them. A great many people would come out and take the whole thing all at one time and just get bombed out of their heads.

Gay, Newmeyer, and Winkler of the Haight-Ashbury Free Clinic also found this to be the case; they say:

> Reared in an era of multiple medication, many of our clients are merely shoppers, wandering from one drug treatment facility to the next, their pockets often bulging with collected pills (downers, or those that "give a buzz" are preferred), as they prepare for the next dry spell of heroin or use the medications directly to supplement the very low potency heroin available on the streets.[28]

In the contemporary drug scene, unlike the heroin world prior to the mid sixties, there are very few pure heroin users, and there are very few periods of total abstinence for addicts. Treatment has intervened to change drug use patterns drastically and the way in which addicts experience the heroin life. I found that most white women who started using heroin in the 1950's were more involved in criminal life—usually before becoming addicted—than those who began to use heroin later; heroin was the only drug they had used, and there was very little poly-drug abuse. The combination of the counterculture, hippie drug scene that produced common use of a host of different drugs—for example, marijuana, cocaine, LSD, speed—and the treatment proliferation with programs offering a host of other drugs—for example, Valium, Talwin, Darvon—has made the woman addict's drug use diverse and continuous.

It has become popular to describe the contemporary heroin addict as a poly-drug abuser,[29] and while the survey population might be called poly-drug abusers, I have discovered that many of the drugs abused in addition to heroin are, indeed, those drugs dispensed at free clinics. This is an interesting irony. Legality alone does not purge drugs of either their euphoric or potentially addictive qualities. In this light, the real differences between legal/treatment and illegal/recreational substances are negligible. It has, in fact, been found that the supposedly medical, therapeutic drugs administered by physicians to troubled middle-class women are contributing to the rise in drug addiction (albeit not heroin) in these women.

"Once a Junkie . . ."

The problems of treatment, addict disillusionment, and subsequent alternative use of the facilities create a situation where there is much recidivism among abstaining women addicts. Indeed, those women in the sample who had been in treatment, had usually participated in several drug rehabilitation programs; their careers were characterized by heroin runs periodically punctuated with treatment. No single modality seemed to be better suited to treating and keeping them away from heroin than any other.[30]

Most women were convinced that getting out of heroin meant physically getting away from other addicts and the heroin world. Coming to a methadone clinic every day is certainly not being removed from the addict social world and can be detrimental to a person committed to doing so. Additionally, the lack of a job makes the task of getting out of the heroin world especially hard. As one woman pointed out:

> People who kick have to have something going for them—school or work. I'm going to go back to school to be a printer and working part-time to keep my time occupied. Even if I'm taking methadone rather than shooting stuff, if there isn't something occupying my time, I'm in trouble. That's the most important thing—keeping your time occupied, keeping your mind busy. And getting away from the addict environment.

Because the structure of both methadone and detox treatment encourages recidivism, these treatment modalities often lock women (and men) into the heroin life. With repeated attempts at abstinence and repeated failures, many women come to believe that it is truly impossible for them to stay clean: "Once a junkie, always a junkie." Such a belief, coupled with the actual reduction of life options, makes it extremely difficult to get out of the heroin life.[31]

Methadone itself can prolong the addict's career in drugs. In the first place, withdrawal from methadone is much more arduous than from heroin, and it takes longer.

> Well, I'm more hooked on that [methadone] than I ever could be on heroin. I've gone through withdrawal and on methadone, it's horrible. I'd take a heroin withdrawal any time.

Secondly, while I found that many women "mature out" of the heroin life by the time they are in their middle 30's, those who have gone on methadone seem to remain on it, thereby continuing their addiction and involvement in the social world of heroin indefinitely; I have yet to talk to a woman who has made a successful break with the heroin life through methadone.

In the straight world, methadone carries the same stigma as heroin addiction, particularly for women. (A woman methadone addict, for example, encounters the same disdain as the woman heroin addict when it comes to employment.) Therefore, in the case of a woman who sincerely wants to be opiate-free and to do, as many women put it, normal things, methadone backfires.

Conclusion

Unlike work and difficulties in taking care of business treatment is one aspect of the heroin life that (except for the obstacle to getting in due to the lack of childcare facilities and sexism in grouping therapy) is similar for men and women. It has become part and parcel of the heroin scene in the last decade. The way that treatment was used by women addicts in this study indicates that it is most often a middle ground between addiction and abstinence. The drugs offered at many treatment facilites are, in fact, used by addicts as a home kicking supply or as recreational drugs. For some addicts, habit control in order to avoid jail or better endure a temporary absence of drugs is the motivation for institutionalized treatment.

Above all, women indicate that they are suspicious of the motives behind the treatment scene and that they find the attitudes within hypocritical. They are, therefore, inclined to regard their own motivation for going to treatment with little seriousness. Consequently, they knowingly use treatment with no sincere attempt at long-term abstinence.

It should be emphasized that treatment facilities can, in fact, be utilized for long-term abstinence if three conditions are met: (1) commitment by the addict to cleaning up, (2) physical removal from opiate-using environments, and (3) availability of an alternative, viable, and desirable lifestyle. One condition without the others is insufficient. A geographically displaced addict will always find heroin if s/he wants it and is not particularly committed to staying clean; a committed person living around other addicts faces too many temptations; even an addict committed to abstinence will drift back to the heroin scene out of loneliness without an alternative social milieu.

The combination of these variables indicates that live-in treatment facilities—either equipped for detoxification or opiate-free—work better than other modalities (out-patient detox and methadone maintenance).[32] For a woman addict, live-in treatment is currently possible only if she has no family commitments; to the 70 percent of the women in this sample who are mothers, treatment facilities without accommodations for children are of no use.

Thus, treatment in its present form does not seem very effective in aiding the woman addict to clean up. The most effective modality would seem to be the therapeutic community[33] that has provisions for children as well as their addicted mothers. But the inability of any treatment center to provide the third crucial variable—a viable and desirable alternative lifestyle—makes successful treatment doubtful at best. As noted by Cuskey et al.:

> For females, the ultimate goals of resocialization and personality reorientation probably will not be realized. The current structure of these modalities does not adequately equip the female with the survival skills necessary for a new drug-free existence and does not significantly alter her basic psychological problems. Even in instances where female ex-addicts remain drug-free for an extended period of time, it seems that treatment has served to detoxify the addict but has been less than successful in preparing her for re-entry into the community.[34]

It is also imperative to have a cure that is no worse than the disease. On methadone, the few social options open to women who have been addicted are further reduced: The woman remains addicted and unable to lead a normal life; the methadone routine ties her to the drug world and other addicts; and her health problems increase dramatically.

If it is necessary to concede that addicts cannot remain opiate-free and that they must, therefore, be maintained on a narcotic in order to reduce drug-related crime, it is necessary to use a drug that is at least no more physiologically, psychologically, and socially harmful than heroin itself.

Until these conditions are met, treatment will continue to contribute to the woman addict's narrowing options. Her failure at abstinence, often brought about by treatment itself, convinces her that she lacks the control necessary to permanently kick heroin. Indeed, she begins to believe that she will always be an addict, and this belief, like narrowing occupational and familial options, ultimately locks her into the heroin world, thus furthering her career in addiction.

CHAPTER EIGHT

Reduced Options

The idea of reduced options is an elaboration of the career concept put forth by sociologists related to the Chicago School. Originally used and developed in the study of traditional occupations and professions, the concept was applied to the sociology of deviance during the 1960's. The model that emerged from this study is closest to the one generally used today, and I have applied it to this study. In order to tie in my own contribution to the career concept, some background on the most important additions to the career concept is in order.

Goffman conceptually extended the career model by introducing the idea of the moral career in *Asylums;*[1] there (and later in *Stigma*) the concept of identity was thoroughly incorporated into the career model.[2] Goffman built upon Lemert's insights into the total self and borrowed the morality component from Tannenbaum's "imputation of evil."[3] Goffman further extended the work of these two authors by treating the concept of career as a link between the individual and social role. Because of the way Goffman cast the moral career, one major consequence was that it became possible for an individual to have a *moral* career simultaneous to his/her career within an institutional setting or social world. Also central to Goffman's scheme was the notion of sequences through time, a theme characteristic of many studies on deviant careers.[4]

Becker's *Outsiders* was both a theoretical contribution to the sociology of deviance and deviant careers and a manifesto of the interactionist perspective.[5] In this work, Becker introduced his notion of career:

> A useful conception in developing sequential models of various kinds of deviant behavior is that of *career*. Originally developed in studies of occupations, the concept refers to the sequence of movements from one position to another in an occupational system made by any individual who works in that system. Furthermore, it includes the notion of "career contingency"—those factors on which mobility from one posi-

tion to another depends. Career contingencies include both objective facts of social structure and changes in the perspectives, motivations, and desires of the individual. Ordinarily, in the study of occupations, we use the concept to distinguish between those who have a "successful" career (in whatever terms success is defined within the occupation) and those who do not. It can also be used to distinguish several varieties of career outcomes, ignoring the question of success.

> The model can easily be transformed for use in the study of deviant careers. In so transforming it, we should not confine our interest to those who follow a career that leads them into ever-increasing deviance. . . . we should also consider those who have a more fleeting contact with deviance, whose careers lead them away from it into conventional ways of life.[6]

The primary importance of Becker's contribution to the study of deviance lies in his development of the labeling process, which is the dimension of the deviant career that, while not necessarily determining further immersion into deviance, illustrates how commitment to deviance is shaped independently of the individual's rule breaking.

By the end of the 1960's, the concept of career had been expanded in many ways. With the appearance of Roth's *Timetables*, the career became organizationally temporalized; with Becker's horizontality, it had already become nonsuccess oriented; and with Goffman's notion of the moral career, the concept became an experience of the self, as Lemert later developed it in "Paranoia and the Dynamics of Exclusion."[7] Despite the new dimensions added to careers in deviance, two properties introduced by Hughes remained constant: fidelity to the investigation and analysis of the intersection of social structure and social-psychology.

The field of social problems had been turned on its head. The root of the problem was seen as lying, not particularly with deviants, but with the agent attempting to correct the problem. The secondary effect of this conceptual shift was an attempt to remove moralization from the analysis of activities that were now to be viewed sociologically with an interested but nonjudgmental eye.

Although the concept of career had been successfully used in the study of deviance (and maybe better than in occupations and professions), careers with explicitly stated diminishing options had not, as yet, been examined. Becker had introduced the notion of horizontality, and this had come the closest to nonprogressive careers; yet, he had used a conventional occupation as his substantive focus. In deviance, too, the assumption was that even if the career were non-conventional, it exemplified the overlap between deviance and convention with its progressive characteristic—that is, one enters the deviant world, gains skills, earns a living, and so forth.

The notion of a career of narrowing options is a novel contribution to the study of careers. It is a backwards progression (perhaps a regression) where, with each step, the individual at once becomes further enmeshed in her/his deviance and further alienated, both socially and psychologically, from conventional life.

The individual enters the career because at the time it appears to offer increased options; s/he makes a commitment to the career (in this study the commitment is addiction); and with this commitment, the option to participate fully in conventional life is not stifled but limited. The commitment to the career increases with further immersion into deviant activities, and eventually, the individual becomes fully inundated—thereby further decreasing the option to go back and forth between both worlds. Next, work activities become centered around the deviant commitment, and these activities serve to limit the possibility of working in the conventional world—an even further narrowing of options. Relationships with family and nondeviant friends become strained, so that options for interpersonal relationships with members outside of the deviant community are reduced.

The recognition of decreasing options often motivates the individual to try to get out of the deviant career. Upon attempting to sustain a conventional lifestyle, the now ex-deviant finds that, indeed, his/her options have been reduced and reentry into nondeviant society proves more difficult than had been assumed. This difficulty is perceived as a personal failure, often causing the individual to retreat back into deviance. What would motivate an individual to reenter a deviant career after having made the necessary (physiological) break with that world? The notion of *reduced* options best explains recidivism in this context.

With each repeated entrance into deviance, the individual becomes more solidly stationed in the deviant world and simultaneously more alienated from conventional life; thus options are slowly narrowing around the deviant. Although the deviant world always seems to await the individual—always alluring, always open—this is deceptive, for with age, the individual is no longer welcome even in this arena. Her/his options have, ironically enough, narrowed in *both* worlds and are completely reduced.

The crucial factor in the deviant career is the length of time one remains. The shorter the time invested in a narrowing career, the better the chance of getting out and investing one's energies in other pursuits. And, quite logically, the longer one stays in such a career, the harder it is to get out and go elsewhere. The career of narrowing options is, then, not absolute, not hopeless, desolate; it is not like quicksand, but depends on commitments, contingencies, and circumstances in the individual's life.

The career of the woman addict is inverted. She begins with somewhat reduced but still viable life options. The longer she remains in the heroin life, however, the more her choices begin to narrow, both objectively and subjectively and primarily in the areas of family and work.

Objectively Reduced Options

Family

The correctional perspective in deviance[8] maintains that deviance per se is inherently pathological but that the deviant can and should be returned to the (conventional and assumed beneficial) fold. In order to do so, it is thought that the deviant must be separated from the deviant world of which s/he is a part.[9] Not surprisingly, many of the objects of correction (I use the term broadly in this context) themselves believe this. A common lament is, "If I could only get out of here (physically), I know I could kick heroin"; in fact, many women's fantasies about abstinence involve traveling to faraway places where heroin cannot be obtained, and no other addicts reside.[10]

After having been addicted for several years, many women envision a heroin-free life married to or living with a nonaddicted man. The man must never have been addicted, because the women believe that anyone who has been addicted (including themselves) can never totally forget heroin. In order, then, to *ensure* abstinence from heroin, they feel that it is necessary to have a partner immune to the heroin yen—a yearning for heroin that addicts often have even after many years of abstinence.

But there is an inherent obstacle to such relationships: Never-addicted men are generally not interested in becoming involved with a woman who has been a heroin addict, convicted of a crime, and probably a prostitute. Thus the option for a relationship with a man who is safe in terms of potential addiction or readdiction is reduced for the woman addict. In most cases, she is forced to limit her relationships to either addicted men or ex-addicts, which could lead to recidivism for her.

Men do not suffer the stigma of addiction as severely as women, especially in the area of interpersonal and sexual relationships.[11] Addicted or formerly addicted men often develop relationships with nonaddicted women, which is many times considered the road to abstinence for men; this rarely works in the reverse however. The woman who has been an addict seems to fall harder than her male counterpart; she alone is defined as "damaged goods." Differentiated societal mores pertaining to men and women are evident here: The man is seen as having temporarily transgressed, whereas the woman is defined as having permanently fallen.

Another reduced option is full-time motherhood. The woman addict's children are often taken away while their mother is incarcerated and placed in foster homes or with relatives. The woman may encounter great difficulty in getting these children back; ironically, she frequently has more trouble with relatives in this regard than with social agencies. Some women give up trying to get their children back and attempt to restructure family life and add to their options by having another baby. It may, however, be impossible for the woman to recreate a family if her childbearing years have ended by the time she matures out of the heroin life.

Work

In the larger society that houses the addict social world, refugees from the criminal-addict world are often deemed occupationally unacceptable; this is particularly true for women. As a group (or caste, as some have labeled it) women have traditionally encountered numerous barriers in the occupational world. In blue collar jobs, where many of the women addicts worked before becoming addicted, the men are awarded the better, high paying positions, while women are relegated to the domestic spheres centering around custodial work and food-related occupations (waitressing). In this kind of work, it is necessary for the woman to interact with customers or employees on a face-to-face basis. The woman ex-addict often has trouble holding down such a job in the conventional world, for as a waitress, secretary, or household helper, she must present herself in a way that is at least moderately appealing to customers and/or employers. Unfortunately, she sometimes has heroin-related scars on her body that cannot be concealed; or her health is poor, and she looks tired and down and out; or she is out of touch with the conventional world and appropriate dress styles for her occupation. Men, on the other hand, who have access to physical labor often do not deal with clientele and, therefore, do not pose a problem to employers if, as ex-addicts, they do not meet the criterion of what the customer wants to see.

Addiction can result in severe health problems. Heroin tends to mask disease symptoms, so that addicted women (and men) may be unaware that they are ill and fail to treat the disease. Moreover, the chaos of the heroin life tends to have a deleterious effect on the addicts' general health. Women often look much older than their age; more important, however, they look and seem *tired* beyond their years. For these reasons women, more than men, have worse employment problems when they attempt to reenter the workforce after having been addicted. Their occupational options are doubly narrowed—as women and as ex-addicts.

The woman addict who is likely to have aged during her chaotic whirl with heroin is apt to find that although her options for success and fulfillment in the conventional world are reduced, she cannot easily retreat to the heroin life: Aging narrows her options in both worlds. Just as the woman's work options are reduced in the non-addict world, so are they in the heroin life. Illegal work requires skills that are very much related to youth; a thief, for example, must possess deftness, speed, and vitality, and a prostitute must be at least somewhat attractive. Furthermore, after a woman has been on the scene for a number of years, she becomes known to law enforcement officials, and illegal work generally becomes more risky for her. Besides having lost job skills necessary in the heroin world, a woman may find it impossible to regain the momentum to function in the chaotic life of addiction. If she is burned-out and tired, heroin is no longer exciting; it is a chore.

Despite all difficulties, the woman addict may, nonetheless, enter the mainstream of society as a productive member. She may find, however, that even after having attained occupational and/or family status she is disappointed and begin to look back at her life in heroin with less disdain. Most probably, she will turn to the euphoria and temporary escape of heroin to alleviate her new problems as an ex-addict. This use, at first sporadic, almost inevitably results in readdiction and reentry into the heroin world. And the cycle of narrowing options will begin anew, each time rendering the woman less able to get out due at least in part, to a subjective reduction of options.

Subjectively Reduced Options

Family

As previously stated, women addicts or ex-addicts are not regarded as desirable by men who have never been addicted, thus forcing these women to choose among other addicts or ex-addicts. This choice is sometimes deliberate, because many women feel that it is difficult to reach intimacy with a partner who either has no understanding of an important aspect of their past life, or could not identify with, condone, or even forgive an involvement with heroin. In this sense, then, women psychologically impose restrictions on their relationships with men.

Often conventional men (as well as ex-addicts) attempt to establish an asymmetric arrangement with the woman in an attempt to carve out a traditional (and hence, it is believed, more solid) relationship. Women who have been active, independent and self-supporting in illegal work find it difficult to enter traditional relationships as the subservient member of a dyad even if they have no leanings toward feminism. These problems with men in general, coupled with a bitterness toward addict-men, who are seen as especially exploitative, make becoming a traditional wife psychologically difficult for the woman addict.

The woman addict may have experienced so much bitterness and resentment toward and from her children as a result of her addiction that her relationship with them is permanently damaged. She may abandon attempts to retain custody of her children, believing that she is unfit or that they have become unmanageable. Occasionally, a woman does not want her children and psychologically relinquishes the option to be a mother.

Work

The woman addict's occupational options are greatly reduced during and after a career in heroin; the difficulty, however, is not totally imposed from without. Identification with the addict life, including illegal work and heroin use, is pervasive. Many women would like to leave the heroin life but are not interested in legitimate work, which is considered low-paying, routine, boring, and too structured; after having fashioned themselves as righteous hustlers, they find it painful to go back to menial, domestic or pink-collar work. As Art Thompson, a San Francisco job counselor, told me recently, "I got this woman a full-time job at McDonalds which paid $700 a month. She told me, 'You must be kidding—$700 a month for a nine-to-five job! I can make $700 a *week* peddling my ass on the street.'" Thus the option for legal work is narrowed by the woman's own preferences.

Reduced Options and Women's Roles

The woman's career in heroin addiction leaves her with objectively and subjectively reduced options both in and out of the heroin life. The woman is excluded from the conventional world, and yet she is unable to function successfully in the heroin world as an addict. Increasingly burned-out, tired, and older, women are forced to choose a substitute narcotic—methadone—and welfare and a Tenderloin hotel room.

The career of narrowing options experienced by the woman addict is particularly ironic in light of the decade of intense change that women in general have seen. The women's movement of the 1970's (and now the 1980's) pushed hard to expand life options for women of all classes. Specifically, it sought to introduce choice into women's lives (as well as men's) by redefining sex and gender roles in a more egalitarian mode than ever before. The social, psychological, and biological ideologies that had fostered and then sustained traditional sex roles, which generally prescribed as ideal the domestic arena for women and more worldly pursuits for men, were attacked. A substitute ideology emerged, where both women and men were seen as fit to participate fully in *both* domestic and worldly affairs. It has become acceptable for women to enter the workforce as full, productive members and/or to raise children.[12] The beauty of these options is that women find it acceptable to partake of either or both—simultaneously or sequentially. In no other period—short of wartime when it was assumed that women's participation in the workforce was temporary—have women had so many options.

Those women who have not benefitted from the destruction of occupational barriers brought about by the women's movement—and this is the case of many working and lower-class women—have at least had the socially integrative and productive option of motherhood (a role often taken for granted). Women addicts lose even this option as their career in heroin progresses and their options regress. Thus, due to the nature of their careers, women addicts experience the opposite of liberation. They are, in fact, more oppressed than other women: They lose not only their work options but their options for a traditional career in wife and motherhood.

While nonaddict women in some sense have more options than men because they can assume domestic roles with social approval, women addicts' situation compared with men addicts' is not parallel—it is worse. As noted, men who have been addicted have the option of doing physical labor, which does not require interpersonal contact. Women have this prerogative less often. Therefore, women ex-addicts are at an occupational disadvantage in comparison to conventional women, men, and formerly addicted men. And they are *also* at a disadvantage with regard to women's traditional roles as mothers because so much interpersonal damage is done to an addict and her family—especially to her children. Thus in speaking of reduced options relative to women's roles, the woman addict paradoxically experiences a narrowing of all conventional options for women—in the home and in the workforce—at a time when role options for women in general have never been greater.

Policy Implications
of Reduced Options

Having explored five dimensions of reduced options—socially reduced options, psychologically reduced options, aging, women's
roles, and the concept of career and reduced options—questions
arise: What are the policy implications of these aspects of reduced options? What practical application can be made to the substantive
focus of this study—women addicts?

Policy implications assumes intervention of some kind; I use the
term to encompass, not only traditional intervention in the form of
arrest, treatment, or incarceration, but job opportunities and family
intervention as well. The timing of any kind of intervention is abso-
lutely crucial for retaining viable life options. The sooner the woman
gets out of the heroin career the less outside options will have been
reduced, and the better her chances for successfully entering the conventional world.

My data overwhelmingly indicates that occupational options are
crucial to women's success in the conventional world. This is no small
matter. The kinds of jobs open to women ex-addicts are often undesirable and impossible to retain due to boredom and insufficient
pay. And the broader economic picture of the 1980's is dismal for
women addicts who are in competition with men and women in a
shrinking job market where keeping it together economically is especially difficult due to inflation.

Secondly, the data point to the importance of women's sense of
success in parenthood as a bond to the conventional world. As in all
classes and subsections of our society, children keep their parents
tuned in to the culture and society, give the parents a broader perspective and often enable them to organize their priorities produc-
tively. Taking away her children is often a destructive gesture for the
addict-mother.

So what should be done? On an individual level the first imperative is education for the woman addict. In this sense I do not mean

formal education but the broadening of perspectives. Narrowness often accounts for a woman's inability to end her career in heroin: She simply knows no other options and does not fully appreciate her own circumstances. It should be made apparent to the woman early that her career is indeed narrowing, that she must, and *can* get out. I do not believe that conversion is necessary, for most women already know that they are on a downward spiral once they have passed the honeymoon stage of addiction. They need encouragement and substantial direction without coercion and without divesting their responsibility and credit for their actions.

In the area of occupational roles, affirmative action should be taken not only in jobs themselves but in preparation for work, such as developing job skills and formal education. Educational projects such as Newgate[1] within correctional facilities and Rebound, a program for ex-convicts at San Francisco State University, should be expanded. Agencies that treat or apprehend women must change their perspectives with regard to women and no longer assume that their roles fall exclusively within the domestic realm and thus, institute useless job training skills in this area. Women must, instead, have access to at least the same occupational training opportunities as their male counterparts.

In terms of jobs themselves, perhaps employers should be given an incentive for hiring women ex-addicts (for example, tax breaks). Such a program could provide a boost to business as well as ex-addicts and would cost the government far less than treating and incarcerating addicts as well as providing foster care for their children.[2]

In an effort to salvage women addicts' roles as mothers, agencies that come into contact with these women must understand the implications of mother-child separation. It is imperative for punitive agencies to provide avenues whereby separation does the least damage, even if this means shorter sentences for women with children. Treatment facilities must incorporate children into their regimens; inhouse centers will have to provide living space for children, and outpatient facilities will have to provide childcare.

In the absence of these changes in occupational and parenting roles, the outlook for women addicts is dismal. But by restructuring addiction careers through social as well as psychological commitment, as hourglasses rather than funnels; by moving individuals into productive work rather than onto welfare; and on an individual level, by respecting drugs, one's own body and adopting nondebilitating health routines the future will not be quite so bleak for these women.

Methodological Procedure

In the following pages, I discuss the research procedure in detail. Although analysis occurred simultaneous to collection, the unique features of research on deviance warrant a lengthier and more detailed discussion of data collection. Because methodological memos and anecdotal material are primarily from the collecting and interviewing phases of research, the relative lengthiness of the discussion of data collection reflects the problematic nature of research on deviance rather than a deliberate emphasis on this phase during the actual project.

Procuring a Sample

Unlike more orthodox grounded theorists, we were contracted through a NIDA-funded research grant to do a specific number of interviews. At the beginning of the project, which was to last two years, the idea of convincing 100 women to consent to do interviews seemed a wild fantasy. How would we find these women? How could we then convince them to come for an interview? How could they be enticed to stay past the $20 remuneration and the vital statistics?

In order to publicize the interviews, the project personnel and I posted printed signs in every conceivable drug community that we knew in San Francisco. The signs read:

WOMEN ADDICTS

We are women interested in learning about women who are addicted to heroin. We are doing a study and are offering *NO* advice, solutions, treatment, or drugs. We need your help and are offering $20.00 payment for your time. All participants are guaranteed confidentiality. Please call us.

921–4987

The sign posting had a dual mission: publicity and field work.

Usually, we parked our car and then canvassed the area for places to post the signs. (We put a sign on any surface that would take a staple.) In so doing, we often drew the attention of the locals, whose reactions were mixed, depending on the racial and ethnic constitution of the neighborhood, the weather, and the quality and quantity of drugs available. We were met with open arms (sometimes quite literally), hostility, disdain, but most of all, curiosity.

The second most popular method of attracting addicts was the lay referral system. We routinely gave calling cards to every woman interviewed and enlisted her help in finding more addicts. We would generally say that we needed a specific number of interviews (however many needed at the time) and ask her to play sociologist. Where would she go to find respondents? What would she do? Many women indicated areas in the city and variations in methods of obtaining respondents that we had not previously considered, and most referred at least one friend to us; some referred six or seven people.

Generally, there was a lull between the time the signs were posted and interviewee response. Regardless of how many lulls we had endured, I still got nervous. After approximately four days, I would be convinced that we had to enlist the help of the two institutions that came into contact with addicts most regularly: jail and treatment. With a little coaxing (and clearance from then-Sheriff Hongisto), the jail authorities and treatment staff allowed us to post our signs in their institutions, which would result in near-havoc for us: At the same time that the street women were beginning to venture in, we were also getting calls from women in jail and treatment.

During the initial interview run, we took everyone. Yet, after a dozen interviews had been completed, I got nervous again, this time for another reason. I felt we should halt the process until we could take stock of the data and begin to sample theoretically; thus, sampling only as new data were needed. And as became evident, with a $20 remuneration, a good reputation on the street, and patience, we could easily procure a sample of 500 if necessary.

It should be noted that the sampling technique yielded a special aggregate of respondents that may not represent the full gambit of addict types. I suspect, for example, that a greater proportion of addicts fall into the upper classes (for example, entertainers, physicians) than are represented by the population surveyed. These addicts are better able to hide their addiction, have no need for the small remuneration offered, but have a great deal at stake if detected. Their addiction careers are quite possibly very different from the more typical poor street addict represented in this study. As a consequence, I make no claims to universality but, instead, limit my generalizations to a population of lower-middle, working, and lower-class women addicts in the San Francisco Bay area at this point in time—the late 1970's.

The Depth Interview

The basic methodological tool employed in this study was the depth interview. Because one of the most important features of the successful depth interview is rapport between interviewer and interviewee, I feared there might be difficulty in enlisting women whose work is very often illegal to do interviews. I, therefore, rented space in the Prisoners' Union building in the Haight-Ashbury district of San Francisco in the belief that housing the project in the Prisoners' Union would remove any suspicions that we were connected with the police. Furthermore, a high drug-using, racially mixed neighborhood was better suited to the project than the institute offices in the Marina district of San Francisco. As it turned out, the interviews could have been held almost anywhere that was accessible to the women: Having had to complete several in the Marina, we learned that drug-using neighborhoods and the Prisoners' Union office building made no difference. We also realized that regardless of how much we tried to pass as the hippest of nonaddicts, we were still taken as straights; however, it didn't make any difference! For reasons that continue to puzzle us, the women, by and large, opened up to us in ways we could never have anticipated. Although we did have elaborate "Protection of Human Subjects" protocol (consent forms that both interviewer and interviewee signed) and routinely gave a short "confidentiality rap" at the beginning of each interview, we could never understand why they trusted us. But they did, and we learned details of their lives that we often could not bear to hear.

The elaborate staging of the comfortable setting may have even backfired in some cases. There were several older women who took the fact that they were being paid to be interviewed very seriously; they had dressed up, were even a little nervous, only to be greeted by a so-called researcher in denim jeans and Birkenstocks. Some felt almost degraded by our casual appearance; they had expected something more scientific.

Interviewee: I have a feeling I'm not saying the things I'm sup-

> posed to say. I thought it was going to be
> scientific.
>
> Interviewer: [laughs] You don't think this is scientific? It
> wasn't scientific enough for you?
>
> Interviewee: It was. It wasn't. I don't know. It was all right. I
> liked it.
>
> Interviewer: Do you have any suggestions for improvement?
>
> Interviewee: No, I'd like to take another interview. I think this
> is fun.

Rapport, we concluded, can work in strange ways. Possibly the fact that we were so obviously not addicts and not part of the heroin world made the women trust us more than if they believed we were involved in drugs. Maybe our naïveté made the women feel that they should elaborate and give us details about their lives and their world. I should also add that during the first six months of interviewing, both the research assistant and I were (very obviously) pregnant, which perhaps made us appear less imposing—somehow more vulnerable and thus easier to relate to. (The women treated us quite gently when we were in this condition, being careful to ask whether their smoking would bother us.) In short, pregnancy seemed to indicate to the women that we were real people, like them, and that we shared female concerns.

The interview itself took the form of a life history. We asked the women to start as far back as they could remember and tell us their life story. We then inquired and probed into areas that most interested us; these areas of interest changed as we continued our theoretical sampling.

There were high points and low points for both the women interviewed and ourselves. For research purposes, the life-history interview (approximately three hours in length) was extremely useful: We were able to see *process* in the lives, stories, and careers of these women and to derive a sense of continuity—to see how events occurred in their lives and, therefore, understand them more fully. Furthermore, by allowing the women to first tell their story in an open-ended fashion, we were able to see which events were most important and significant *to them*. We were occasionally surprised to learn that their use of heroin—the focus of *our* study—was not of major import in their lives relative to other concerns.

The depth interview has the potential to net the researcher massive amounts of data and information; it can also be less than productive, particularly if theoretical sampling has not been utilized effectively. Although the researcher has the power to choose her/his sample in the attempt to elicit new and necessary information, another variable—the astuteness of the respondent—cannot always be guaranteed. Occasionally, fellow researchers or other interviewees referred us to a woman who "could really talk," "was really smart," or "had really been through a lot." These known key informants are rare and most of the time, you take your chances.

We came up with a humorous typology of interviewees, admittedly beginning with our favorites and ending with those types who were most difficult to interview. We were always delighted when we found that we were interviewing the natural sociologist; she did our work for us, and everyone appreciates that. These women were concise, clear, articulate, abstract, worldly, and able to analyze their own situation and the broader problem of opiate addiction. Many of these types had been in treatment and gone through therapy; some had college experience; a few were political, and many were just bright. Our next favorite was the "entertainer." These women were lively, funny, sometimes outrageous, always animated. We had to work harder with them, but the session was always productive and kept us on our toes; it made our sociological tasks quite pleasant. We interviewed several "flippy ladies," many of whom were addicted to methadone. These interviews were an exercise in stream of consciousness for them. They either paid little attention to the questions or digressed on irrelevant subjects (which seemed to last for hours) or forgot their point mid sentence. Then there was "the bitch": Such women were hostile, monosyllabic, ready to take the money and leave immediately. We had arguments and exchanged insults with some of them. Finally, there was the "sad lady." These women could point to nothing redeeming about their lives, their futures; they often cried and brought us to tears also. After one of these interviews, we needed a martini and a few days of lapse time before going out in the field again.

The depth interviews provided us with the bulk of our data; their value to us is obvious. Of late, with Protection of Human Subjects concerns, the question of exchange has entered discussions of using interview subjects. Just what did we give to them? Frankly, I'm not sure at this point that it wasn't an equal exchange. Since the project was federally funded, we were able to pay the respondents $20 in cash; but that wasn't all. We felt we almost provided a service for these women: Their worlds are so inundated by heroin and other addicts that we were often the only nonaddicts with whom they could talk. The interview provided a change in their lives—a different experience from the usual hustling and using cycle. As noted earlier, the paid interview made the women feel important; they were being paid to share some of their knowledge and expertise rather than being "therapized," and they appreciated this. Finally, the interview offered the women a chance to reflect on their lives and their futures; to think about things they had never considered. Some women hoped that their contribution might have an impact on their own lives and particularly their children's. As one woman said:

> Interviewer: So, why did you come for the interview?
> Interviewee: 'Cause I was so curious, and, like I said, I'm interested in the female addict anyway because I am one. And I want to know where all this is gonna go. Like, will it be better for me later on? Maybe will it be better for somebody else I know? What if I have a child? You know, I have a little girl somewhere. What if she uses? And, like, later on in life, will she be able to get a job? Will she be able to fit into society? Will she have a better understanding? Will my son be able to accept me when I tell him? He already knows I'm going to a clinic, and he knows there's something else going on, like, I'm sick a lot. I don't feel well. He doesn't know why. He has an idea, I'm sure.

Depth interviewing also has its low points—both for the interviewer and interviewee, and interviewing deviants can compound the usual problems. For example, most of the women interviewed were poor; all other reasons aside, they came to be interviewed because they needed the money. We faced this quite early. Some women needed the money so badly that they came to the interview in the midst of a bout of withdrawal sickness; they fidgeted and one woman even vomited during the interview. On the other hand, some women came for the interview right after they had fixed, and they simply nodded out. Methadone can produce a similar effect, so the women on methadone either nodded or became incapable of finishing a sentence until reminded of what they were saying. Thus, there was always a strain on the interviewer to keep the interview going. The research assistant had, however, a sure way of getting the woman interested again—talking about drugs; it always picked things up. A disproportionate number of addicts smoke cigarettes and smoke heavily, so that in a small interviewing room, a nonsmoking researcher can almost literally become sick (especially one who is pregnant). Finally, several women had to bring their children. The presence of the children was often less distracting and disheartening than their condition when they were dirty, not dressed warmly enough, and hungry.

Scheduling interviews with addicts is extremely difficult. Due to the chaotic nature of the heroin world we had to be available immediately if a woman wanted to be interviewed. In the beginning, we tried to schedule the interviews as though we were running a dentist's office; we soon found this didn't work. If the woman was still hooked, we had to interview her immediately; if on methadone or in treatment, we could make an appointment a day or two in advance; and if she was clean, we could schedule her as much as three days in advance. Even with this plan, 30 percent of the scheduled interviewees never showed up or called; another 10 percent didn't show up for their first or second appointment but were subsequently interviewed.

Other problems with scheduling interviews included being hustled by the women. Occasionally, two women would come in together when only one interviewer was available; naturally, they both wanted the money even if one was willing to forego the interview. Many women brought their spouses, and we had to occupy their time for two to three hours. Less often, a woman would have less than an hour to spare, in which case we simply said that the interview took much longer and would have to be postponed (without paying the money, of course). We were met with pleas of poverty, sickness, and the assurance that she could tell her entire story in 15 minutes. One woman was interviewed for three hours, and when I paid her $20, she became indignant. She claimed she had been told the payment was $20 for *every 15 minutes* that she stayed!

Depth interviewing people in desperate and sad situations can be emotionally draining for both the respondent and the interviewer, especially since many of the women had led impoverished lives prior to their current situation and had little hope for the future. In addition, all the interviewers (myself, the research assistant, and secretary) are mothers and wives, which made us especially sensitive to those areas of the women's lives that often caused them the most pain—their children and spouses.

An inherent problem with questioning individuals about their experience—past and present—is retrospection: Do the subjects rewrite their experience to suit their present condition and justify themselves to a nonaddict interviewer. In more formal methodological terms this situation is referred to as the problem of validity. There are three conditions that neutralized the problem of retrospection for us: present addiction, interviewing technique, and rapport. The majority of the women interviewed (80 percent) were using some opiate—either heroin or methadone or both—at the time of the interview; therefore, their reports were not wholly retrospective but a current account of their lives and lifestyle. The study of presently addicted street women was, in fact, designed to reduce common problems of retrospection. Secondly, our interviewing technique made fashioning an ideology or justification very difficult. We attempted to move in chronological order and were successful at keeping the interviewee on the track. We noted discrepancies in stories and were not reluctant to probe, question, and call attention to such discrepancies. Any false biography would have had to have been rehearsed and well planned, and we doubted that these women had the time or motive for fantasy. Furthermore, since we used the snowball method, we were able to crosscheck their accounts and did find them reliable. Lastly, as noted earlier, our casual style enabled us to gain rapport with the women in a relatively short period of time. Characteristically we revealed at the outset our own neutral perspective on drug use in general and sometimes give the women details about our own drug experimentation; we became real people to these women—people who didn't have a stake in discrediting them and who were not out to judge their past and present involvement in drugs. I must mention that the vast majority of the life histories were so pathetic that it is difficult to imagine anyone making them up: They were neither grandiose, self-congratulatory, nor condemning but what seemed to be honest accounts of real experience.

One last problem with depth interviewing were the entreaties.[1] In attempting to befriend and take the women into our confidence, we were faced with dilemmas. We sincerely did not know the ethical, moral, and practical limits of our obligations. Several women hinted at their need for money; one couple actually borrowed money from me. I was sure they would pay me back, since they said that the check was coming the next day and they just needed the money to buy food. Occasionally, a woman wanted a recommendation from us to get into a treatment program, which made us wonder about the validity of the interview just completed. The research assistant was asked her advice on childcare after a woman had been arrested. One woman liked our project so much that she asked for a job. Finally, a woman who wanted to have her welfare payments increased asked (when I was eight-months pregnant) if she could submit my urine specimen to prove to the welfare agency that *she* was pregnant.

It is important to note that even with the problems encountered, none of the stereotypical notions of the dangerous dope fiend were ever realized; our experience was similar to Lindesmith's in this area.[2] Nothing was ever stolen from us, even when we had to leave the room (and purse) to use the facilities or make coffee, no bodily harm came to us or was ever threatened. While in the interview setting, the women showed respect for us, our work, and themselves and were, by and large, extremely polite to us as well as considerate.

In addition to the depth interviews, we did a fair amount of field work. Although several male ethnographers have done much field work with addicts in urban centers as part of their research, we found that as women we were limited. We felt especially vulnerable, since we were less equipped to defend ourselves physically than a man might be. Given the focus of our investigation—women, who do not spend a great deal of time on the streets—we needed entree into their homes and few women were willing to give us this kind of leeway. We were outsiders to their world; therefore, even if they trusted us, our presence would threaten their status. Furthermore, I should note that social research is not welcomed with open arms in the drug-using community; when we were welcomed, it was because our contacts expected remuneration.

The risk and chaos of the heroin world also impeded our field work. I was able to accompany a (male) friend and occasional user on his rounds in the heroin community where my presence never ceased to be a curiosity to his associates and, I suspect, a discomfort to him. I simply was not an addict, and my appearance did not allow me to blend in to the scenery naturally. I did have one chance to visit a shooting gallery as a nonparticipant, but as will happen in the heroin world, the place was busted two hours before I arrived.

In sum, the problems of doing field work in drug communities— the vulnerability of women researchers, the relative secrecy of women addicts, and the suspicion aroused by field workers—made us rely much more heavily on our depth interviews in collecting and analyzing data.

Analysis

Analysis was done simultaneously with data collection. Directly after each interview, the interviewer recorded instant impressions of the session: a full description of the physical, social, and personal characteristics of the respondent; where the woman fit in our scheme; and future areas for exploration based on the data gathered in this interview. The interview was then transcribed and coded. The codes continually evolved, as they were based on what seemed to be the most salient aspects of the data. For example, we found from the outset that mothering and motherhood were important categories from the number of times these topics were mentioned by the respondent.

After an interview was coded, a memo was prepared, which consisted of theoretical, observational, and methodological notes about a particular subject area from the data that had been coded in this area. The memos, which varied in length, were always based on some aspect of the data under analysis and provided direction for further theoretical sampling, since they inevitably led to questions that needed answering; for example, does this phenomenon occur with blacks as well as whites; how does age affect this aspect of the heroin life; do women raised in high drug areas use at a younger age?

As previously indicated, problems of scheduling interviews made elaborate theoretical sampling quite difficult. We had what is known in some drug-research circles as an "opportunity sample." Our own theoretical sampling was twofold: We restructured our interview schedule bimonthly; we asked the respondents new sets of questions about subject areas that we wanted to explore. In addition, we sampled what we considered to be diverse and differing populations of women; for example, we went on missions to get certain groups— blacks, Latinas, older women. (26-year-old, white women on methadone seemed to be omnipresent.) At one point, we felt it was important to learn about the differences between incarcerated and nonincarcerated women, so we invaded the jails; the same occurred with treatment. Later, we tried to stay away from women in jail and treatment and concentrated on the streets. In short, the sampling varied with the findings that were emerging in the already collected data.

Saturation was reached after half the interviews were completed. At this point, I felt theoretically satisfied; it was time to start writing. Yet, we still had 50 interviews to complete. We used the remaining interviews to (1) verify the emerging theory and (2) insure racial and ethnic representativeness in an attempt to cover ourselves if confronted by quantitative-type analysts who are sometimes more concerned with sample than theory. We shifted the focus of the interview to what we had already discovered about women and addiction. The new interviewees added to our theory, were exceptions to parts of it, and occasionally uncovered an aspect of the phenomenon that we had not taken into account, which proved extremely useful as a validating device. We also conducted several sessions with three or four women at a time as a further validating device. Since the women tended to become more analytic and less personal in a group setting as opposed to an individual interview, these sessions were not only valuable but quite enjoyable for us.

Almost at the outset, five areas emerged as most important in analyzing this data: getting in, the heroin world, work, love and parental relationships, and treatment. Each had a major part in the narrowing of options that is the basic social process in the career of the woman addict. The writing proceeded when I felt each area was saturated, based on the thoroughness and continuity of the memos, which were filed according to codes and sorted into more elaborate categories that organized my work. Consequently, writing difficulties occurred for emotional or personal reasons rather than due to problems with the data and its organization.

And I did experience difficulties. Occasionally, I became so immersed in the substantive aspects of the analysis that I temporarily lost sight of the theoretical direction. The intervention of Strauss and Schatzman at various points forced me to take stock of my analysis and integrate the substantive aspects of my work into the general theory.

Two different subject areas presented me with problems while writing. I was confronted with phenomenological inadequacy in attempting to explain the social-psychological aspects of becoming addicted. My objective was to take the reading audience with me down the path of addiction, so they could fully understand why and how women become heroin addicts, yet my lack of personal experience as an addict made me feel inadequate in this endeavor. I never resolved this. I had another type of problem while writing about motherhood. The data were so disturbing that I had frequent emotional breakdowns; at various points, I doubted I could continue.

The organization afforded by the grounded theory perspective and method enabled the rest of the research to proceed smoothly. Above all, the writing provided me with an intense sense of satisfaction and the accomplishment of proposing a theory that might explain, illuminate, and generally make sense out of the careers of women heroin addicts.

Demographic Statistics

To complement the depth interviews, we collected quantifiable data on demographic aspects of the survey population. A summary statement describing the tables follows.

Summary

Age (Table 1)

While there was a broad age spectrum (20–53 years of age), over half of the women (59 percent) were under 30. Nearly one quarter of the survey population (19 percent) were under 25. Twenty-eight percent of the women were in their 30's and 13 percent were over 43.

Race (Table 2)

The survey population was split nearly equally between white (43 percent) and black (38 percent) women. We also interviewed 14 Latinas, 1 Asian, 1 native American, and 3 Filipinos.

Geographical Location of Childhood (Table 3)

Over half (51 percent) of the population sampled came from San Francisco (35 percent) or the San Francisco Bay area (16 percent); the other 49 percent came from a variety of cities all over the country.

Parents' Occupation (Table 4)

The largest single category of father's occupation was blue collar (34 percent). A sizable number (23 percent) did not know their father's occupation because there had been no contact with him. Thirteen percent of the fathers had white-collar occupations, and 13 percent had illicit occupations (for example, pimping) or were usually

unemployed. The other categories were menial (7 percent), professional (5 percent), and military (3 percent).

One third of the women's mothers (32 percent) had been homemakers; 20 percent were in pink-collar occupations; 17 percent in
menial jobs; 6 percent in clerical; 6 percent in professional work; 5
percent in illicit occupations such as prostitution; and 1 percent of the
women claimed that they did not know their mother's occupations or
refused to answer.

Religion (Table 5)

The largest single group of respondents (37 percent) stated they
were Catholic. Twenty-nine percent of the women were Protestant,
and 28 percent claimed they had no religion. We interviewed one
woman who was Jewish, one Muslim, and four who were other re-
ligions or refused to answer.

Length of Addiction (Table 6)

The modal length of addiction was seven years (51 percent). One
fourth of the population sampled (25 percent) had been addicted less
than four years and 29 percent over ten years. Ninety-four percent
had been addicted at least three years.

Family Members Addicted (Table 7)

Nearly half (44 percent) of the women had family members (mother, father, sibling, child, aunt, uncle, or cousin) who had been addicted. One fifth (20 percent) of the survey population had two or
more addicted family members, and 13 percent had three or more.

Education (Table 8)

Thirty-seven percent of the population sampled had not finished
high school. Thirty-two percent were high school graduates (often
getting their diplomas in prison); and one fourth (25 percent) had
had some college. Three percent had graduated from college, and the
others (3 percent) refused to answer or did not know.

Juvenile Arrests (Table 9)

The survey population was divided almost equally on juvenile arrests; 51 percent had been arrested as juveniles and 49 percent had not.

Employment (Table 10)

Nearly half (45 percent) of the population sampled had never held down a job. One fifth (19 percent) had been employed in clerical positions; 10 percent in the bar and restaurant businesses; 9 percent in domestic work; 12 percent in blue and pink-collar jobs; and 4 percent in illicit occupations such as working in massage parlors.

Hustles (Table 11)

Many of the women (88 percent) reported at least three hustles in which they participated, therefore, the total number of hustles equals 230. Two thirds of the population sampled (61 percent) reported having dealt drugs intermittently, and an almost equal number (60 percent) had been involved more regularly in prostitution. Twenty-eight percent of the women had been shoplifters; 21 percent forgers; 18 percent burglars; 17 percent robbers; 6 percent bag-followers and 6 percent con women; 5 percent pickpockets and 3 percent auto thieves; 1 woman was a pimp; and 4 women had never hustled at all.

Time Served (Table 12)

Seventy-eight percent of the survey population had served some time in jail or prison. Twenty-six percent of the population sampled (the single largest group) had served three months or less. A little over three fifths (62 percent) had served three years or less, and only 16 percent had served more than three years.

Marital Status (Table 13)

Most of the women (77 percent) were not married. Thirty-four percent were single; 24 percent divorced; 4 percent widowed; and 15 percent separated. Only 23 percent of the population sampled was currently married.

Sexual Orientation (Table 14)

The majority of the women (82 percent) were heterosexual. Ten percent were bisexual and 8 percent homosexual.

Children (Table 15)

Seventy-two percent of the population sampled had children. Most (51 percent) had one or two children; 28 percent had no children; and 21 percent had three or more.

Table 1. Age at the Time of the Interview

Age in years	Frequency percent (n)	Cumulative frequency percent
20–24	19.0 (19)	19.0
25–29	40.0 (40)	59.0
30–34	19.0 (19)	78.0
35–40	9.0 (9)	87.0
43–53	13.0 (13)	100.0
Total	100.0 (100)	

Table 2. Race

Race	Frequency percent (n)
White	43.0 (43)
Black	38.0 (38)
Latin	14.0 (14)
Asian	1.0 (1)
American Indian	1.0 (1)
Filipino	3.0 (1)
Total	100.0 (100)

Table 3. *Geographical Location of Childhood*

Location	Frequency percent (n)
San Francisco	35.0 (35)
Bay area	16.0 (16)
Other (assorted)	49.0 (49)
Total	100.0 (100)

Table 4. *Parents' Occupation*

Father's Occupation	
Occupation	Frequency percent (n)
Blue-collar	34.0 (34)
Unknown	23.0 (23)
White-collar	13.0 (13)
Illicit	9.0 (9)
Menial	7.0 (7)
Professional	5.0 (5)
Usually unemployed	4.0 (4)
Military	3.0 (3)
Refused	1.0 (1)
Total	100.0 (100)

Mother's Occupation	
Occupation	Frequency percent (n)
Homemaker	32.0 (32)
Pink-collar	20.0 (20)
Menial	17.0 (17)
Unknown	13.0 (13)
Clerical	6.0 (6)
Professional	6.0 (6)
Illicit	5.0 (5)
Refused	1.0 (1)
Total	100.0 (100)

Table 5. Religious Background

Religion	Frequency percent (n)
Catholic	37.0 (37)
Protestant	29.0 (29)
None	28.0 (28)
Other	3.0 (3)
Jewish	1.0 (1)
Muslim	1.0 (1)
Refused	1.0 (1)
Total	100.0 (100)

Table 6. Length of Addiction

Years	Frequency percent (n)	Cumulative frequency percent
1	2.0 (2)	2.0
2	2.0 (2)	4.0
3	10.0 (10)	14.0
4	11.0 (11)	25.0
5	8.0 (8)	33.0
6	6.0 (6)	39.0
7	12.0 (12)	51.0
8	17.0 (17)	68.0
9	3.0 (3)	71.0
10	6.0 (6)	77.0
11–15	14.0 (14)	91.0
18–30	9.0 (9)	100.0
Total	100.0 (100)	

Table 7. Addicted Family Members[a]

Number of addicted family members	Frequency percent (n)
0	56.0 (56)
1	24.0 (24)
2	7.0 (7)
3	13.0 (13)
Total	100.0 (100)

[a] Addicted family members: mother, father, sibling, child, uncle, aunt, cousin.

Table 8. Education

Years of education	Frequency percent (n)	Cumulative Frequency percent
Not grade school graduate	4.0 (4)	4.0
Some high school	33.0 (33)	37.0
High school graduate	32.0 (32)	69.0
Some college	25.0 (25)	94.0
College graduate	3.0 (3)	97.0
Refused	1.0 (1)	98.0
Unknown	2.0 (2)	100.0
Total	100.0 (100)	

Table 9. Juvenile Arrests

Juvenile arrests?	Frequency percent (n)
Yes	51.0 (51)
No	49.0 (49)
Total	100.0 (100)

Table 10. Employment History

Job[a]	Frequency percent (n)
Never worked	45.0 (45)
Clerical	19.0 (19)
Bar-restaurant	10.0 (10)
Domestic work	9.0 (9)
Pink-collar	8.0 (8)
Illicit	4.0 (4)
Blue-collar	4.0 (4)
Other[b]	1.0 (1)
Total	100.0 (100)

[a] Employment: holding a job for three months or longer.

[b] "Other": a woman who worked as an art therapist.

Table 11. Summary of All Hustles Reported

Hustles	Count	Percent of cases
Dealing	61	61.0
Prostitution	60	60.0
Boosting[a]	28	28.0
Forgery	21	21.0
Burglary	18	18.0
Robbery	17	17.0
Bag-following	6	6.0
Bunco-con	6	6.0
Pickpocket	5	5.0
Did not hustle	4	4.0
Auto theft	3	3.0
Pimp	1	1.0
Total	230[b]	230.0

[a] Shoplifting.
[b] Eighty-eight percent of the sample reported at least three hustles, therefore, total hustles reported is 230.

Table 12. Jail and Penitentiary Time Served

Time served	Frequency percent (n)	Cumulative frequency percent
None	22.0 (22)	22
3 mo. or less	26.0 (26)	48
4–12 mo.	18.0 (18)	66
1–2 yr.	12.0 (12)	78
2–3 yr.	6.0 (6)	84
3–5 yr.	7.0 (7)	91
5–8 yr.	5.0 (5)	96
10+ yr.	4.0 (4)	100
Total	100.0 (100)	

Table 13. Marital Status

Marital status	Frequency percent (n)
Single	34.0 (34)
Married	23.0 (23)
Divorced	24.0 (24)
Separated	15.0 (15)
Widowed	4.0 (4)
Total	100.0 (100)

Table 14. Sexual Orientation

Orientation	Frequency percent (n)
Heterosexual	82.0 (82)
Homosexual	8.0 (8)
Bisexual	10.0 (10)
Total	100.0 (100)

Table 15. Total Number of Respondents' Children

Number of children	Frequency percent (n)	Cumulative frequency
0	28.0 (28)	28.0
1	27.0 (27)	55.0
2	24.0 (24)	79.0
3	7.0 (7)	86.0
4	8.0 (8)	94.0
5	4.0 (4)	98.0
6	2.0 (2)	100.0
Total	100.0 (100)	

Glossary

(*Compiled by Sheigla Murphy, with the assistance of Sharon Harsha and Marsha Rosenbaum.*)

This glossary has been included to help the reader understand the terms and phrases used by our respondents; it is by no means a comprehensive listing. The definitions apply, for the most part, to the context(s) in which the reader finds them. In consulting other glossaries of addict argot, we were amazed at the number of words that were popular in Lindesmith's era (the 1940's) and are still in use today—often with only a slight variation in meaning.[1] Many of these terms are also part of the vernacular of the prison culture, the music scene, and more generally, the youth culture.

Bag (n.) Container of narcotics, especially heroin (which is often sold in balloons or plastic bags); hence a supply of narcotics.

Bag-follower (n.) Also bag-bitch; bag-broad; bag-bride. A woman who exchanges sexual favors in return for heroin; women who live or associate with dealers in order to be near a constant supply of heroin. (Men and women alike denigrate this type of woman. Unlike a prostitute, who is paid in money for sexual services, the bag-follower barters sexual favors for heroin; this is an important distinction in the addict world.)

Blow it (v.) To make a mistake consciously or unconsciously. More generally, to lose control of one's actions due to drug effects; for example, "I guess I must have been really blowing it, because the next thing I knew, I was in jail." "Blowing it" also means getting angry, losing control of one's emotions; for example, "He hit me and then I really blew it. I just went crazy and started hitting him."

Boosting (n.) Shoplifting.

Broad (n.) Woman; also bitch, chick.

Build up (one's habit—v.) To increase daily drug dosage.

Bunk (n.) Poor quality drugs; for example, "I came here to buy some heroin, but this stuff is bunk." A lie, untruth, bullshit.

Burn (v.) To sell poor quality drugs or a substance that does not contain any of the drug it is represented to be.

Bust (n.) Arrest.

Changes (Go through changes—n. phr.) Problems and difficulties encountered; for example, "You go through so many changes trying to score heroin." (See also "Hassle.") Turning points, personal life events that change or transform the person.

Chippy (n./v.) 1. One who uses heroin a little but is not addicted. 2. To use heroin occasionally; for example, "I chippied for three months before I was addicted."

Clean (adj.) Not under the influence of opiates. A user is considered clean if s/he doesn't have any drugs on her/his person or premises.

Cold turkey (adv.) To stop using drugs suddenly, without tapering off, or without using other drugs for relief. To kick a habit cold turkey.

Con (v./adj.) 1. To elicit a victim's *con*fidence in order to take money; to swindle. 2. Con games are stylized, illegal tricks used by hustlers to defraud victims, such as the Murphy game—a con game in which a victim is sent to a nonexistent prostitute but is told to leave all his money and other valuables with the con man's partner, Miss/Mrs. Murphy.

Connection (n.) One who sells drugs; also a dealer.

Cooker (n.) 1. The receptacle (usually a spoon) in which drugs are dissolved and heated prior to being drawn up into the hypodermic syringe or outfit. 2. In the cooker means using heroin.

Cool (adj.) In *Junkie*, Burroughs writes: "Cool, an all-purpose word indicating anything you like or any situation that is not hot with the law. Conversely, anything you don't like is 'uncool'" (p. 120). More currently: Good, popular.

Cop (v./v.i.) 1. To purchase drugs. To admit something. 2. To obtain something (usually illegal or improper).

Cotton (n.) A small piece of cotton through which the drug solution is strained into the syringe in order to strain out foreign matter that might clog the needle.

Crackdowns (police—n.) Intensive police attention to particular areas and particular kinds of crimes.

Crash pad (n.) A pad is one's home; to crash is to go to sleep. A place where people (often runaways) can sleep on the floor; often a house where hippies live.

Croaker (n.) A doctor.

Cut (v./n.) 1. To adulterate drugs. 2. The substance used to adulterate the drug.

Date, dating (n.) The prostitute's customer; trick. Dating is the act of prostitution; also hoeing.

Deal (v.) To sell illegal drugs.

Dealer (n.) One who sells illegal drugs. (See "Connection.")

Dirty (adj./n.) 1. Having illicit drugs in one's possession. 2. A urine sample with evidence of illicit drugs.

Dog (n.) An unattractive or ugly woman. (See "Low-life.")

Dope fiend (n.) A drug addict; user, junkie, hype.

Down and out (adj.) Poor and depressed.

Dude (n.) Man.

Dynamite (adj.) Usually powerful or pure drugs. A very good thing, for example, "That band plays dynamite music."

Fence (n.) One who buys and sells stolen goods.

Fix (v./adj.) 1. To take drugs; for example, "I want to fix very soon." To take enough drugs to relieve abstinence symptoms; for example, "Two bags in the morning and I'm fixed." 2. In a nondrug context, satisfied; for example, "I only eat one meal and I'm fixed."

Fucked up (adj.) Having made a big mistake. Too full of a drug to enjoy its full effects; incapacitated.

Get down (v.) 1. To inject heroin. 2. To have intercourse.

Habit (n.) Being addicted. A habit is described in temporal as well as monetary terms; for example, "My first habit lasted two years." "I have a $50-a-day habit."

Hanging out (n. phr.) Socializing; on the scene.

Hassle (n.) Problems and difficulties. (See "Changes.") Fights or disagreements, verbal or physical.

Heart (*have the heart*—n.) Drive, motivation, guts; for example, "Once I went to the penitentiary, I just didn't have the heart to be forging checks anymore."

High (adj.) Under the influence of drugs; loaded, stoned, wasted.

Hoeing (n.) Whoring; also dating, turning tricks, hooking.

Holding your mud (v. phr.) Conducting oneself appropriately, especially keeping your business to yourself; not informing the police.

Hooked (adj.) Addicted; strung out. To have used drugs long enough so that withdrawal symptoms appear upon cessation.

Hooker (n.) Prostitute.

Hot (adj.) A person who is liable to attract attention from the law. A place watched by the police.

Hustle (v.) To engage in the illicit and illegal activities of the addict and/or criminal subcultures. To move quickly.

Hustler (n.) Participant in illicit and illegal activities.

Hype (n.) Originally, one who used a hypodermic needle; now used interchangeably with junkie, addict, dope fiend, user.

Jack (v.) To let the medicine dropper or syringe fill with blood, then inject the blood into the vein after injecting the drug solution in order to enhance the rush experienced from injecting.

Jones (n.) Habit.

Junk (n.) Opiates, especially heroin; also dope, stuff, brown, downtown.

Junkie (n.) A drug addict; hype, dope fiend, user.

Kick (v.) To overcome, especially a narcotics habit.

Loaded (adj.) Full of drugs; under the influence of drugs; also high, stoned, fucked up, wasted.

Low-life (adj./n.) A person or action considered extremely undesirable due to its unscrupulousness; for example, "You can't let those low-life motherfuckers in your home, they'll steal your toothpaste."

Make (v.) To con. To get something through deceit or manipulation; for example, "That doctor over there on Haight Street, I made him for 100 Valiums."

Making it (n. phr.) Keeping it together, surviving; making enough money to meet survival needs (food, shelter, staying out of jail); buying enough heroin to keep from being sick and maybe even getting high.

Mess with (v.) To have intercourse with; for example, "The dude I was messing with had some good dope." To have contact with; for example, "I don't mess with drugs anymore."

Monkey on my back (n. phr.) A habit.

Motherfucker (n.) A person (not necessarily pejorative).

Nod (v.) To experience a euphoric, drowsy, dreamy state from narcotics use; also coasting. Addicts on the nod look like they are sleeping, but they are in fact aware of their surroundings.

O. D. (v.) To overdose; to lose consciousness.

Oil-burning (adj.) A large, costly habit; for example, "When I was dealing dope, I had an oil-burning habit."

Old man/old lady (n.) Wife/husband or woman/man that one is having a relationship with. A woman might refer to her husband or the man she lives with as *my old man*.

Outfit (n.) A user's outfit for injecting heroin; also *works, fit*. Consists of a medicine dropper, hypodermic needle, a spoon or other container in which to dissolve the heroin.

Outlaw (n.) One outside the law.

Register (v.) To allow the blood to appear in the lower portion of the medicine dropper when making an injection in order to indicate that the needle is in the vein.

Right guy—all right (n./adj.) An addict who is not an informer or who will not act as an informer when arrested; for example, "You can sell to her, she's all right."

Rip off (v.; *Rip-off*, n.) 1. To steal. 2. A thief.

Run (n.) The length of time one uses a particular drug. A run is measured from the first injection after a nonusing period to the last injection before an abstinent period.

Score (v./n.) 1. To make a purchase, buy drugs, make a connection, cop. To obtain something (usually illegal or improper; for example, heroin). 2. Money and goods obtained through hustling activities.

Script (n.) Prescription.

Shoot (v.) To inject (narcotics); to fix.

Shooting gallery (n.) A place where users meet to inject drugs.

Sick (adj.) In need of narcotics; suffering withdrawal from narcotics; ill. In bad taste.

Skin pop (v.) To inject drugs into the skin intramuscularly rather than intravenously.

Sleazy (adj.) A person or action that is underhanded, unreliable, shabby, cheap, unprincipled.

Snort (v.) To inhale powdered drugs.

Snorter (n.) One who snorts drugs.

Speed ball (n.) Cocaine and heroin used together.

Spoon (n.) Roughly a teaspoon (actually much less); equivalent to four $20 bags or balloons of heroin.

Square (n.) A nonaddict.

Stash (v./n.) 1. To hide something (usually heroin or other illegal drugs). 2. Dope that has been secreted; for example, "I found her stash and took it."

Stoned (adj.) Under the influence of drugs; also *high, loaded, wasted*.

Straight (adj./n.) 1. A feeling of normalcy. An addict is straight when not experiencing withdrawal; for example, "I needed to do two bags to get straight." 2. One who is not a user. (See also "Squares.") 3. One who is not homosexual.

Street (n./adj.) The public areas where addicts and hustlers congregate. Working the street refers to prostitutes who walk the pavement searching for potential customers. A prostitute who sees herself in a higher socio-economic bracket will say, "I never worked the street. I had regular customers." 2. Street drugs are drugs that can be purchased from sellers who are known to hang out on a certain corner at a particular time. Street heroin is often considered to be of inferior quality to heroin purchased from a connection who has a place (apartment, hotel room) to sell from. The seller of street heroin is a street dealer and is on the lowest rung of the selling hierarchy, selling highly adulterated heroin. Street addicts are those addicts who spend most of their time on the street, living a hand-to-mouth, poverty-stricken existence, suffering withdrawal symptoms. In the areas of the buying and selling of heroin, lifestyle, and prostitution, the further removed one is from the actual sidewalk, the further up the social scale one is.

Strung out (adj.) Addicted, hooked.

Taking care of business (n. phr.) Fulfilling obligations. Often pertains to obligations surrounding a heroin habit as well as more conventional obligations like paying the rent.

The life, The fast life (n.) Somewhat dated term best described by Wepman et al. in *The Life*: "The Life has been variously defined: the world of prostitution, the world of drug addiction, the entire 'culture of poverty.' But the life is both more and less than these" (p. 2).

The man (n.) Law enforcement official.

Tie up (v.) To distend one's veins by applying an improvised tourniquet.

To turn out (v. phr.) To introduce someone to heroin. To cause someone (through persuasion, coercion) to become a prostitute; for example, "When I was 16, he turned me out. I've been turning tricks since then."

Tracks (n.) Marks or scars from hypodermic injection of narcotics.

Trip (n.) A psychedelic experience. A person's "thing," "schtik," beliefs, or practices.

Try to get next to (v. phr.) To attempt to have sexual relations with; for example, "He tried to get next to me, and I told him it was going to cost him some money."

Turn on (v.) To take drugs. To introduce someone to drug use; for example, "I turned her on to some of my cocaine."

Turning tricks (n. phr.) Tricks are a prostitute's customers. Practicing prostitution; also dating, hoeing, hooking.

Wake up (n.) First injection of the day; for example, "I needed a wake up to get going in the morning."

Wasted (adj./v.) 1. Under the influence; also high, loaded, stoned. 2. To waste someone is to kill the person.

Working girls (n.) Prostitutes.

Works (n.) Instruments used in taking an injection.

Write (v.) To give a prescription for drugs that can be sold or used to ease withdrawal symptoms.

Yen (n.) The desire for narcotics; describes the longing for narcotics experienced by people who are not currently addicted to heroin; for example, "I've been clean for six months, but then I ran into some people I used with before and that old yen hit me again."

Notes

Chapter One

1. See B. Ehrenrich and D. English, *Complaints and Disorders*; J. S. Haller and R. M. Haller, *The Physician and Sexuality in Victorian America*; C. Smith-Rosenberg, "The Hysterical Woman," pp. 652–678.
2. See C. E. Terry and M. Pellens, *The Opium Problem*; T. Duster, *The Legislation of Morality*.
3. R. L. Dupont, "Drugs, Alcoholism, and Women."
4. L. Richards, "The Epidemiology of Youthful Drug Use."
5. Refer to G. Blinick, C. Wallach, and E. M. Jerez, "Pregnancy in Narcotic Addicts Treated by Medical Withdrawal," p. 997; G. Blinick, E. M. Jerez, and R. G. Wallach, "Methadone Maintenance, Pregnancy, and Progeny," p. 477; M. A. Pelose, M. Frattorola, and J. Apuzzio, "Pregnancy Complicated by Heroin Addiction," p. 512; J. F. Perlmutter, "Drug Addiction in Pregnant Women," p. 569; J. L. Rementeria, S. Janakammal, and M. Hollander, "Multiple Births in Drug Addicted Women," p. 958; P. Rothstein and J. B. Gould, "Born With a Habit"; S. S. Stoffer, "A Gynecologic Study of Drug Addicts," p. 779; M. L. Stone, L. J. Salerna, and M. Green, "Narcotic Addiction in Pregnancy," p. 716; C. Zelson, "Infant of the Addicted Mother," p. 26.
6. See J. Densen-Gerber, M. Weiner, and R. Hochstedler, "Sexual Behavior, Abortion, and Birth Control in Heroin Addicts," p. 783; L. P. Finnegan, J. F. Connaughton, and J. P. Emich, "Comprehensive Care of the Pregnant Addict and Its Effect on Maternal and Infant Outcome," p. 795.
7. See G. DeLeon, "Phoenix House," p. 135; E. H. Ellinwood, W. G. Smith, and G. E. Vaillant, "Narcotic Addiction in Males and Females," p. 33; J. S. Miller et al., "Value Patterns of Drug Addicts as a Function of Race and Sex," p. 4; D. Waldorf, *Careers in Dope*.
8. For example, C. Chambers et al., "Narcotic Addiction in Females," p. 257; J. E. Williams and W. M. Bates, "Some Characteristics of Female Narcotic Addicts," p. 245.
9. W. R. Cuskey, A. D. Moffet, and H. B. Clifford, "A Comparison of Female Opiate Addicts Admitted to Lexington Hospital in 1961 and 1967," pp. 89–103.
10. See R. Baldinger, B. M. Goldsmith, and W. G. Capel, "Pot Smokers,

Junkies, and Squares," p. 153; C. E. Climent et al., "Epidemiological Studies of Female Prisoners," p. 345.

11. See C. Chambers and J. Inciardi, "Some Aspects of the Criminal Careers of Female Narcotics Addicts"; P. T. d'Orban, "Heroin Dependency and Delinquency in Women," p. 67; K. N. File, T. W. McCahill, and L. D. Savitz, "Narcotics Involvements and Female Criminality," p. 177; J. James, "Female Addiction and Criminal Involvement"; J. C. Weissman and K. N. File, "Criminal Behavior Patterns of Female Addicts," p. 6.

12. Refer to C. A. Eldred and M. M. Washington, "Female Heroin Addicts in a City Treatment Program," p. 75; C. Gioia and R. Byrne, "Distinctive Problems of the Female Drug Addict," pp. 531–538; B. J. Kaubin, "Sexism Shades the Lives and Treatment of Female Addicts," p. 471; S. J. Levy and K. M. Doyle, "Attitudes toward Women in a Drug Abuse Treatment Program," p. 428; L. Ponsor, E. Soler, and J. Abod, "The ABC's of Drug Treatment for Women"; A. Schultz, "Radical Feminism," pp. 484–502.

13. See I. Chein et al., *The Road to H*; M. Rosenbaum, "Sex Roles among Deviants," (Forthcoming); Waldorf, *Careers in Dope*.

14. H. M. Hughes (Ed.), *The Fantastic Lodge*.

15. J. Prather and L. Fidell, "Drug Use and Abuse among Women," pp. 863–885.

16. J. Ball and C. Chambers, *The Epidemiology of Opiate Addiction in the U.S.*; Chein, *The Road to H*.

17. As noted by Densen-Gerber, "Sexual Behavior in Heroin Addicts," p. 783; James, "Female Addiction."

18. F. Suffet and R. Brotman, "Female Drug Use," pp. 19–23.

19. S. Christenson and A. Swanson, "Women and Drug Use," p. 4.

20. A. Schutz, *Collected Papers, Vol. I*.

21. G. H. Mead, *Mind, Self, and Society*.

22. H. Blumer, *Symbolic Interactionism*.

23. E. Goffman, *Asylums*, p. 127.

24. B. Glaser and A. Strauss, *The Discovery of Grounded Theory*.

25. B. Glaser, *Theoretical Sensitivity*.

26. L. Schatzman and A. Strauss, *Field Research*.

27. For a more detailed description of the methodological process and composition of the sample, the reader should refer to Appendix II.

Chapter Two

1. For a closer look at these studies see M. Agar, *Ripping and Running*; H. Feldman, "Ideological Supports to Becoming and Remaining a Heroin Addict," pp. 131–139; S. Fiddle, *Portraits from a Shooting Gallery*; L. C. Gould et al., *Connections*; P. Hughes et al., "The Social Structure of a Heroin Copping Community," pp. 551–558; E. Preble and J. Casey, "Taking Care of Business," pp. 1–24; A. Sutter, "The World of the Righteous Dope Fiend," pp. 177–182.

2. See J. James, "Prostitution and Addiction," pp. 601–618.

3. A. Lindesmith, A. Strauss, and N. Denzin, *Social Psychology*, p. 514.

4. See P. Biernacki, *The Social Careers of Heroin Addicts*; I. Chein et al., *The Road to H*; D. N. Nurco et al., "Studying Addicts over Time," pp. 183–196; J. O'Donnell, "Lifetime Patterns of Narcotic Addiction"; G. Vaillant, "The Natural History of Narcotic Drug Addiction," pp. 486–498; D. Waldorf, *Careers in Dope*; C. Winick, "Some Aspects of Careers of Chronic Heroin Users."

5. See H. Alksne, L. Lieberman, and L. Brill, "A Conceptual Model of the Life Cycle of Addiction," p. 2; L. Robins, *Addict Careers*; E. Rubington, "Drug Addiction as a Deviant Career," p. 2.

6. See S. Fiddle, "Sequences in Addiction," pp. 553–567.

7. See M. Agar, *Ripping and Running*; Feldman, "Ideological Supports," pp. 131–139; Gould, *Connections*; H. Hendler and R. Stephens, "The Addict Odyssey," pp. 25–42; Preble and Casey, "Taking Care of Business," pp. 1–24; M. Ray, "The Cycle of Abstinence and Relapse among Heroin Addicts," pp. 132–140; Sutter, "The World of the Righteous Dope Fiend," pp. 177–182; R. Weppner, "An Anthropological View of the Street Addict's Worlds," pp. 111–121.

8. It should be noted that addiction careers vary: Not every addict goes through each of these phases. Few individuals, however, bypass the initial stage of becoming an addict. Of those who do become addicts, some stay at a maintaining phase (perhaps the most competent); others only maintain for a short period before they reach the conversion phase. In short, the addiction career model is an abstraction and should be regarded as such.

9. The convict code, according to J. Irwin in *The Felon*, prohibits one convict from reporting another to authorities.

Chapter Three

1. A. Lindesmith, A. Strauss, and N. Denzin, *Social Psychology*, p. 174.

2. J. Irwin, *Scenes*, p. 65.

3. For a complete analysis of the hippie trip see S. Cavan, *Hippies of the Haight*; L. Yablonsky, *The Hippie Trip*; Irwin, *Scenes*.

4. Irwin, *Scenes*.

5. For a complete discussion of this phenomenon see H. Schwendiger, *The Insiders and the Outsiders*.

6. See S. Murphy, "A Year with the Gangs of East Los Angeles."

7. For an excellent description and analysis of the ghetto see C. Brown, *Manchild in the Promised Land*; I. Slim, *Pimp*.

8. See E. Liebow, *Tally's Corner*.

9. H. Finestone, "Cats, Kicks, and Color," p. 286.

10. F. Adler, *Sisters in Crime*, p. 87.

11. See A. Y. Cohen, "Inside What's Happening," pp. 2092–2095; V. A. Dohner, "Motives for Drug Use," pp. 317–325; D. J. Feldman and H. S.

Feldman, "On the Etiology of Narcotic Addiction and its Relation to Curiosity," pp. 304–308; M. Keeler, "Motivation for Marijuana Use," pp.
142–146; K. Keniston, "Heads and Seekers," pp. 97–112; G. L. Mizner et
al., "Patterns of Drug Use among College Students," pp. 15–24.

12. See R. Coombs et al. (Eds.), *Socialization in Drug Abuse.*
13. H. Blumer et al., *The World of Youthful Drug Use,* p. 173.
14. See B. S. Brown et al., "In Their Own Words," pp. 635–645; I. Chein et
al., *The Road to H;* H. Hendler and R. Stephens, "The Addict Odyssey,"
pp. 25–42.
15. See H. Feldman, "Ideological Supports to Becoming and Remaining a
Heroin Addict," pp. 131–139; Fiddle, "Sequences in Addiction," pp.
553–567; Murphy, "Gangs of East Los Angeles."
16. Many women reported that they felt surrounded by drugs since childhood, and one indication of this is that over half (52 percent) had family
members who had been addicted.
17. See D. Gerstein et al., "Career Dynamics of Female Heroin Addicts";
M. Rosenbaum, "Sex Roles among Deviants" (Forthcoming); D. Waldorf, *Careers in Dope.*
18. W. Burroughs, *Junkie,* p. xv.
19. D. Matza, *Becoming Deviant.*
20. See C. Chambers, *An Assessment of Drug Use in the General Population;*
J. O'Donnell et al., *Young Men and Drugs;* R. Scharse, "Cessation Patterns among Neophyte Heroin Users," pp. 23–32.
21. T. Duster, *The Legislation of Morality,* p. 70.
22. Rosenbaum, "Sex Roles among Deviants," (Forthcoming).
23. See H. Alksne, L. Lieberman, and L. Brill, "A Conceptual Model of the
Life Cycle of Addiction," p. 2.
24. It is interesting to note that today's "head shops" (boutiques that carry
drug paraphernalia) stock an assortment of goods. As part of the main
stock displayed in windows and on shelves, one can find pipes for
smoking marijuana and hashish; clips to hold a marijuana cigarette; devices to clean marijuana; "stash" boxes to store marijuana; cocaine kits
with gold razors to chop cocaine; mirrors with the word "cocaine" writ-
ten on the front for cutting cocaine; spoons and straws for snorting cocaine. I once browsed in such a shop for a long period of time, admiring
the vastness of the stock and chuckling at what I considered to be the
boldness of displaying such obvious and illegal drug paraphernalia. I
commented to the salesman on the wide array of devices available and
asked if he sold works—a term used to refer to heroin paraphernalia.
The man looked at me aghast; more surprised, I am sure, that I should
ask than that I might possibly be a user. This experience supported my
feeling that the division between hard and soft, the narcotic and counterculture drug world is, indeed, great.
25. See J. Howard and P. Borges, "Needle Sharing in the Haight," pp.
220–230.
26. H. Becker, "Becoming a Marijuana User," pp. 235–242. Becker also

noted that the experienced marijuana user gets high much faster than the novice, because prior use accelerates the effects of the drug.

27. See A. Lindesmith, *Addiction and Opiates.*
28. See N. Zinberg and W. Harding, "The Effectiveness of the Subculture in Developing Rituals and Sanctions for Controlled Drug Use."
29. See D. Wepman, R. Newman, and M. Binderman, *The Life.*
30. Irwin, *Scenes*, p. 28.
31. Wepman, *The Life*, pp. 167–169.

Chapter Four

1. R. Broadhead, "Inundation of Family Life."
2. A dealer runs the risk of being "ripped-off" by the clientele. For two interesting discussions of clientele rip-off, see M. Moore, *Buy and Bust*; P. A. Adler and P. Adler, "The Irony of Secrecy in the Drug World," pp. 447–467.
3. See M. Agar, *Ripping and Running*; H. Finestone, "Cats, Kicks, and Color"; E. Preble and J. Casey, "Taking Care of Business," pp. 1–24.
4. Although the term "dope fiend" and especially "righteous dope fiend" has neutral to positive connotations for the addicted man (see J. Irwin, *The Felon* and D. Waldorf, *Careers in Dope*), the term "dope fiend broad" carries negative connotations.
5. For an excellent discussion of being and doing see N. Chodorow, "Being and Doing."
6. A. Trocchi, *Cain's Book*, p. 73.
7. See Moore, *Buy and Bust.*
8. A. Goldman and L. Schiller, *Ladies and Gentlemen, Lenny Bruce!*, pp. 6–7.
9. T. Duster suggested that in order to get a measure of the women's inundation by the heroin world, I should ask the interviewees to estimate the percentage of addicts living in San Francisco. Indeed, while the actual figure is purported to be about 1 percent (NIDA, 1978; as reported in the *San Francisco Chronicle*, April 7, 1978), the women tended to make estimates from 50 to 80 percent!
10. See P. Hughes et al., "The Social Structure of a Heroin Copping Community"; W. McAuliff and R. Gordon, "A Test of Lindesmith's Theory of Addiction," pp. 795–840; A. Sutter, "The World of the Righteous Dope Fiend," pp. 177–182.
11. See Sutter, "The World of the Righteous Dope Fiend," pp. 177–182.
12. See S. Fiddle, *Portraits from a Shooting Gallery*; J. Larner and R. Tefferteller, *The Addict in the Street.*
13. The nature of the master status is described by E. Hughes, "Dilemmas and Contradictions of Status," pp. 353–359.
14. R. H. Blum and Associates, *The Dream Sellers.*
15. Trocchi, *Cain's Book*, p. 73.

Chapter Five

1. See T. Caplow, *The Sociology of Work*.
2. For an example of the way in which sociologists have looked at crime as work see P. Letkemann, *Crime as Work*.
3. G. Miller, *Odd Jobs*, pp. 239–240.
4. See H. Becker and A. Strauss, "Careers, Personality, and Adult Socialization," pp. 253–263; R. Blauner, *Alienation and Freedom*; E. Chinoy, *Automobile Workers and the American Dream*; E. Hughes, *Men and Their Work*; R. M. Kanter, *Men and Women of the Corporation*; W. Moore, "Occupational Socialization"; S. Terkel, *Working*.
5. For a more complete discussion of this process see H. Becker, *Outsiders*; E. Goffman, *Asylums* and *Stigma*; E. Lemert, *Social Pathology*; J. Lofland, *Deviance and Identity*; D. Matza, *Becoming Deviant*.
6. See M. Agar, *Ripping and Running*; J. Irwin, *The Felon* and *Scenes*; E. Preble and J. Casey, "Taking Care of Business," pp. 1–24; D. Waldorf, *Careers in Dope*.
7. J. O'Donnell, "Lifetime Patterns of Narcotic Addiction," p. 245.
8. Waldorf, *Careers in Dope*, p. 50.
9. For discussions of opportunity and drift see, respectively, R. Cloward and L. Ohlin, *Delinquency and Opportunity*; D. Matza, *Delinquency and Drift*.
10. Some notable studies on the relationship between crime and addiction are contained in I. Chein et al., *The Road to H*; J. James, "Prostitution and Addiction," pp. 601–618; A. Lindesmith, *Addiction and Opiates*.
11. H. Hughes (Ed.), *The Fantastic Lodge*, p. 192.
12. For a complete discussion of this perspective see Matza, *Becoming Deviant*.
13. For discussions of criminal careers see H. Shaw, *The Natural History of a Delinquent Career*; E. Sutherland, *The Professional Thief*; Letkemann, *Crime as Work*; Miller, *Odd Jobs*; M. Rosenbaum and B. Rosenblum, "A History of the Concept of Career in Sociology."
14. See Preble and Casey, "Taking Care of Business," pp. 1–24; B. Sackman et al., "Heroin Addiction as an Occupation," p. 2; Waldorf, *Careers in Dope*.
15. I use the term "odd job" differently than Miller, who refers to the entire spectrum of deviant work as an odd job in his book *Odd Jobs*. However, in his only reference to addicts, Miller discusses the lowest type of thief, the junkie, and says, "This thief is the least skilled of the types. . . . his stealing is generally spontaneous, and he tends to steal objects that are easily available and often of little value" (p. 43). While junkie work is sporadic, deviant work as described by Miller is occupational in style.
16. See J. Mortimer and J. Lorence, "Work Experience and Occupational Value Socialization."
17. See R. Ball and J. R. Lilly, "Female Delinquency in an Urban County," pp. 279–281; C. Chambers et al., "Narcotic Addiction in Females,"

p. 257; W. R. Cuskey, "Survey of Opiate Addiction among Females in the United States Between 1850 and 1970," pp. 8–39; J. Densen-Gerber et al., "Sexual Behavior, Abortion, and Birth Control in Heroin Addicts," p. 783; C. A. Eldred and M. M. Washington, "Female Heroin Addicts in a City Treatment Program," p. 75; E. H. Ellinwood et al., "Narcotic Addiction in Males and Females," p. 33; S. Fiddle, "Sequences in Addiction," pp. 553–567; K. N. File et al., "Narcotic's Involvements and Female Criminality"; Goldstein, *Prostitution and Drugs*; C. Chambers and J. Inciardi, "Some Aspects of the Criminal Careers of Female Narcotics Addicts"; James, "Prostitution and Addiction," pp. 601–618; M. Rosenbaum, "Sex Roles among Deviants," (Forthcoming); A. Sutter, "The World of the Righteous Dope Fiend," pp. 177–182; J. C. Weissman and K. N. File, "Criminal Behavior Patterns of Female Addicts," p. 6; L. Yablonsky, *Synanon*; M. Zahn and J. Ball, "Patterns and Causes of Drug Addiction among Puerto Rican Females," pp. 203–214.

18. James, "Prostitution and Addiction," pp. 601–618.
19. See N. Davis, "The Prostitute."
20. E. Goode, *Deviant Behavior*, p. 334.
21. P. Biernacki, C. Kaplan, and M. Rosenbaum, "Junkie Work," (Forthcoming). According to this work, identity and self-concept are largely dependent upon the status of the hustle within the world of deviant work. My argument is that entrance into illegal work in general is crucial to identity.
22. T. Duster, *The Legislation of Morality*, p. 211.
23. The California Rehabilitation Center is a facility for the incarceration of offenders with a drug history or drug-related conviction.

Chapter Six

1. For a discussion of this aspect of addiction see G. DeLeon and H. K. Wexler, "Heroin Addiction," pp. 36–38.
2. See D. Wellisch, G. Gay, and R. McEntee, "The Easy Rider Syndrome," pp. 425–430.
3. See D. Waldorf, *Careers in Dope*, pp. 159–177.
4. See L. Rubin, *Worlds of Pain*.
5. See E. Liebow, *Tally's Corner*.
6. See B. Sackman et al., "Heroin Addiction as an Occupation," p. 2.
7. Rubin, *Worlds of Pain*, p. 176.
8. M. Komarovsky, "Cultural Contradictions and Sex Roles," p. 256.
9. For discussions of the centrality of motherhood see J. Bardwick and E. Douvan, "Ambivalence"; J. Bernard, *The Future of Motherhood*; N. Chodorow, *The Reproduction of Mothering*; N. Weisstein, "Psychology Constructs the Female."
10. See G. Blinick, "Fertility of Narcotics Addicts and Effects of Addiction on the Offspring," pp. S34–S39; E. C. Gaulden et al., "Menstrual Abnormalities Associated with Heroin Addiction," pp. 155–160; R. Hertz,

"Addiction, Fertility, and Pregnancy," pp. S40–S41; R. Wallach, "Pregnancy and Menstrual Function in Narcotics Addicts Treated with Methadone," pp. 1226–1229.

11. C. Winick, "Epidemiology of Narcotics Use."

12. See E. M. Brecher, *Licit and Illicit Drugs*; A. Lindesmith, *Addictions and Opiates*; C. Sheppard, D. Smith, and G. Gay, "The Changing Face of Heroin Addiction in the Haight-Ashbury," p. 122.

13. For an excellent discussion of crimes without victims see E. Schur, *Crimes without Victims*.

14. See G. Blinick et al., "Pregnancy in Narcotics Addicts Treated by Medical Withdrawal," pp. 997–1003; R. L. Naeye et al., "Fetal Complications of Maternal Heroin Addiction," pp. 1055–1061; J. L. Rementeria and N. N. Nunag, "Narcotic Withdrawal in Pregnancy," pp. 1052–1056; P. Rothstein and J. B. Gould, "Born with a Habit," pp. 307–321.

15. H. Schneck, "Narcotic Withdrawal Symptoms in the Newborn Infant Resulting from Maternal Addiction," p. 585.

16. For lengthy discussions of this phenomenon see Blinick, "Pregnancy in Narcotics Addicts," p. 997; L. P. Finnegan, "Narcotics Dependency in Pregnancy"; and S. K. Krase, "Heroin Addiction among Pregnant Women and Their Newborn Babies," pp. 754–758.

17. With a moderate drug dose some women can function normally, even optimally. Many women reported that when using heroin they had the ability to do housework and care for their children in ways that far exceeded their nondrugged state. One woman said:

> Taking care of the baby was hell, especially if I ain't got nothin' [heroin]. I feel bad because I have to keep laying him down there and I just feed him his bottle and then after that I say, "I can't just keep doing that." So, I try to get up, but I'm not really up to playing with him or nothin'. Then, finally, when I get my fix, I seem like I'm a whole different person. I could take care of him and take care of the house and still have more time.

18. See Bernard, *The Future of Motherhood*; Chodorow, *The Reproduction of Mothering*.

19. See E. Preble and J. Casey, "Taking Care of Business," pp. 1–24.

20. See B. S. Brown et al., "In Their Own Words," pp. 635–645; M. Rosenbaum, "Sex Roles among Deviants," (Forthcoming).

Chapter Seven

1. See J. Inciardi, *Methadone Diversion*; E. Preble and T. Miller, "Methadone, Wine, and Welfare"; D. Waldorf, *Careers in Dope*.

2. T. Wolfe, *Radical Chic and Mau-mauing the Flak Catchers*, p. 168.

3. C. Winick, *Some Comments on Consequences of Chronic Opiate Use*, p. 236.

4. For discussions of this philosophy see M. Jones, *Beyond the Therapeutic Community*; G. Nash, "The Sociology of Phoenix House"; R. Völkman

and D. Cressey, "Differential Association and the Rehabilitation of Drug Addicts," pp. 129–142; L. Yablonsky, *Synanon*.

5. R. G. Newman, *Methadone Treatment in Narcotic Addiction*.
6. See D. Nelkin, *Methadone Maintenance*.
7. Personal conversation, October 1978.
8. See W. R. Cuskey, L. Berger, and J. Densen-Gerber, "Issues in the Treatment of Female Addiction," pp. 307–371; S. K. Ruzek, "Report to the California State Office of Narcotics and Drug Abuse Prevention and Treatment of Female Drug Dependency."
9. The author has no independent data on staff drug use. The accusations were made by several women, and it might be argued that only the unsuccessful exaggerate this phenomenon in order to excuse their own inability to abstain. It should also be noted that the data presented in this chapter reflect the women's perspective on treatment. Further study is necessary in order to present treatment staff's perspective.
10. See C. Chambers et al., "Physiological and Psychological Side Effects Reported during Maintenance Therapy"; W. A. Bloom and B. T. Butcher, "Methadone Side Effects and Related Symptoms and 200 Methadone Maintenance Patients."
11. R. Hempden-Turner, *Sane Asylum*.
12. J. Ball et al. had similar findings. They report that although treatment staff saw the patient as mentally and physically sick, the addict saw him/herself as neither. See J. Ball et al., "The Heroin Addict's View of Methadone Maintenance," pp. 89–95.
13. See M. Burt et al., *An Investigation of Outcomes of Traditional Drug Treatment/Service Programs*; M. Colton, "Descriptive and Comparative Analysis of Self-perceptions and Attitudes of Heroin Addicted Women"; S. J. Levy and K. M. Doyle, "Attitudes toward Women in a Drug Treatment Program," pp. 423–434; E. Soler et al., "Women in Treatment."
14. See C. Chambers et al., "Narcotic Addiction in Females," p. 257; I. Chein et al., *The Road to H*; G. DeLeon, "Phoenix House," p. 135; F. Glaser, "Narcotic Addiction in the Pain-prone Female Patient," p. 2.
15. See Soler, "Women in Treatment"; Levy, "Women in a Drug Treatment Program"; L. White, "It Isn't Easy Being Gay."
16. J. Reichart and R. Klein, *An American Way of Dealing*.
17. Preble, "Methadone, Wine, and Welfare," p. 233.
18. G. W. Joe et al., *An Evaluative Study of Methadone and Drug Free Therapies for Drug Addiction*, pp. 71–72.
19. See Burt, *Traditional Drug Treatment/Service Programs*.
20. Joe, *Methadone and Drug Free Therapies*, pp. 71–72.
21. For in-depth discussions of the way that women are perceived by physicians and psychiatrists, see P. Chessler, "Patient and Patriarch"; K. Lennane and R. Lennane, "Alleged Psychogenic Disorders in Women," pp. 288–292; N. Weisstein, "Psychology Constructs the Female."
22. See L. S. Brahen, "Housewife Drug Abuse," pp. 13–24; R. Cooperstock, "Sex Differences in the Use of Mood-modifying Drugs," pp. 238–244;

H. Lennard, *Mystification and Drug Misuses*; H. J. Parry, "Patterns of Psychotropic Drug Use among American Adults," pp. 269–273.

23. See M. Balter and J. Levine, "The Nature and Extent of Psychotropic Drug Usage in the U.S.," pp. 12–24; Cooperstock, "Mood-modifying Drugs," pp. 238–244; Parry, "Psychotropic Drug Use." Of late, there has been increasing alarm in the medical world about the newly discovered extent of housewife drug abuse. Indeed, a large population of sedative addicts has been created by the physician's perspective and treatment of women's medical complaints. For an interesting discussion of this problem see L. S. Linn and M. S. Davis, "The Use of Psychotherapeutic Drugs by Middle-Aged Women," pp. 331–340.

24. See W. R. Cuskey, "Survey of Opiate Addiction among Females in the U.S. Between 1850 and 1970," pp. 8–39.

25. Waldorf, *Careers in Dope*, p. 92.

26. See H. Alksne et al., "A Conceptual Model of the Life Cycle of Addiction," p. 2.

27. K. Carlson, "Treatment as Perceived by the Addict," pp. 569–584.

28. G. Gay, J. A. Newmeyer, and J. J. Winkler, "The Haight Ashbury Free Medical Clinic," D. M. Smith and G. Gay (Eds.), *It's So Good, Don't Even Try It Once* (Englewood Cliffs, NJ: Prentice Hall, 1972), p. 82.

29. See Sackman et al., "Heroin Addiction as an Occupation," p. 2.

30. This was also discovered by Macro-Systems, Inc., *Three Year Follow-up of Clients Enrolled in Treatment Programs in New York City*; and Burt, *Traditional Drug Treatment/Service Programs*.

31. See M. Ray, "The Cycle of Abstinence and Relapse among Heroin Addicts," pp. 132–140.

32. Burt, *Traditional Drug Treatment/Service Programs*.

33. See W. E. Aron and D. Daily, "Short and Long-term Therapeutic Communities," pp. 619–636; J. Marsh and R. Neely, *Women Helping Women*.

34. Cuskey, "Treatment of Female Addiction," p. 342.

Chapter Eight

1. See E. Goffman, *Asylums*.

2. See E. Goffman, *Stigma*.

3. See E. Lemert, *Social Pathology*; F. Tannenbaum, *Crime and the Community*.

4. See J. Roth, *Timetables* for a systematic development of the temporal dimension of career.

5. For a complete discussion of the interactionist perspective see E. Sagarin, *Deviance and Deviants*.

6. H. Becker, *Outsiders*, p. 24.

7. H. Becker, "The Career of the Chicago Public School Teacher," pp. 44–77; E. Lemert, "Paranoia and the Dynamics of Exclusion," pp. 2–20.

8. See D. Matza, *Becoming Deviant*.

9. The therapeutic community and the parole system are built upon these

premises, and their policies with regard to clients reflect this persuasion.

10. D. Waldorf and P. Biernacki have also shown this to be the case in their study of natural and therapeutic recovery from heroin addiction. Many addicts feel that physical removal from the heroin world or any proximate place (for example, the city) is necessary for abstinence; thus the desire for the country.

11. In fact, J. Irwin (personal conversation, 1980) notes that male "exes" (ex-convicts, ex-addicts) are seen as attractive by some women. Evidence of this is their willingness to marry incarcerated men, as detailed by N. Meredith in her recent article "Romance Blooms at San Quentin," *California Living*, Magazine of the San Francisco Sunday Examiner and Chronicle, October 19, 1980. Also, the assumed boldness or toughness of men who have done time is seen as attractive. The anti-hero in *Urban Cowboy* is an example of this kind of attraction.

12. Although the new ideology has supported the same dual role options for men, hesitancy to enter the domestic arena on a full-time basis coupled with the current economic crunch and inflation has kept men nearly exclusively in the breadwinning role.

Appendix I

1. For a detailed description and analysis of these programs see M. J. Seashore et al., *Prisoner Education*.

2. In point of fact, the Federal Revenue Act of 1978 has created new federal funds to assist ex-offenders convicted of felonies through a targeted job tax credit. Employers who hire ex-offenders can attach a new IRS form to their tax returns for a tax credit of up to 50 percent of the first $6,000 in the first year of wages and 25 percent of the same during the second year.

Appendix II

1. For a description of entreaties, see J. Irwin, "Participant Observation of Criminals."

2. See A. Lindesmith, *Addiction and Opiates*.

Appendix IV

1. See the glossaries in W. Burroughs, *Junkie*; A. Lindesmith, *Addiction and Opiates*; D. Wepman, R. B. Newman, and M. Binderman, *The Life*.

Bibliography

Adler, F. *Sisters in Crime*. New York: McGraw-Hill, 1975.

Adler, P. A., and Adler, P. "The Irony of Secrecy in the Drug World." *Urban Life: A Journal of Ethnographic Research*, 8 (1980):447–467.

Agar, M. *Ripping and Running: A Formal Ethnography of Urban Heroin Addicts*. New York: Seminar, 1973.

Alksne, H., Lieberman, L., and Brill, L. "A Conceptual Model of the Life Cycle of Addiction." *International Journal of the Addictions*, 2 (1967): 221–239.

Aron, W. E., and Daily, D. "Short and Long-term Therapeutic Communities: A Followup and Cost-effectiveness Comparison." *International Journal of the Addictions*, 9 (1974):619–636.

Baldinger, R., Goldsmith, B. M., and Capel, W. G. "Pot Smokers, Junkies and Squares: A Comparative Study of Female Values." *International Journal of the Addictions*, 7 (1972):153.

Ball, J., and Chambers, C. *The Epidemiology of Opiate Addiction in the U.S.* Springfield, IL: Thomas, 1970.

Ball, J. H., Graff, M., and Sheehan, J. J. "The Heroin Addict's View of Methadone Maintenance." *British Journal of the Addictions*, 69 (1974):89–95.

Ball, R., and Lilly, J. R. "Female Delinquency in an Urban County." *Criminology*, 14 (1976):279–281.

Balter, M., and Levine, J. "The Nature and Extent of Psychotropic Drug Usage in the U.S." *Psychopharmacology Bulletin*, 5 (1969):12–24.

Bardwick, J., and Douvan, E. "Ambivalence: The Socialization of Women." In V. Gornick and B. Moran (Eds.), *Woman in Sexist Society*. New York: Basic Books, 1971.

Becker, H. "The Career of the Chicago Public School Teacher." *American Journal of Sociology*, 57 (1951):44–77.

———. "Becoming a Marijuana User." *American Journal of Sociology*, 59 (1952):235–242.

———. *Outsiders*. New York: The Free Press, 1963.

Becker, H., and Strauss, A. "Careers, Personality and Adult Socialization." *American Journal of Sociology*, 62 (1956):253–263.

Bernard, J. *The Future of Motherhood*. New York: Penguin Books, 1974.

Biernacki, P. *The Social Careers of Heroin Addicts*. San Francisco: Institute for Scientific Analysis, 1973. (Final report, NIMH Grant #R01 DA 00280)

Biernacki, P., Kaplan, C., and Rosenbaum, M. "Junkie Work: The Social Hierarchy in the World of Heroin." *Journal of Drug Issues*, Forthcoming.

Blauner, R. *Alienation and Freedom*. Chicago: University of Chicago Press, 1964.

Blinick, G. "Fertility of Narcotics Addicts and Effects of Addiction on the Offspring." *Social Biology*, 18 (1971):S34–S39.

Blinick, G., Wallach, C., and Jerez, E. M. "Pregnancy in Narcotic Addicts Treated by Medical Withdrawal." *American Journal of Obstetrics and Gynecology*, 105 (1969):997–1003.

Blinick, G., Jerez, E. M., and Wallach, R. G. "Methadone Maintenance, Pregnancy and Progeny." *Journal of the American Medical Association*, 225 (1973):477.

Bloom, W. A., and Butcher, B. T. "Methadone Side Effects and Related Symptoms and 200 Methadone Maintenance Patients." *Proceedings of the Third National Conference on Methadone Treatment*, 1971. (Mimeographed)

Blum, R. H., and Associates, *The Dream Sellers*. San Francisco: Jossey-Bass, 1972.

Blumer, H. *Symbolic Interactionism*. Englewood Cliffs, NJ: Prentice-Hall, 1969.

Blumer, H., Sutter, A., Smith, R., and Ahmed, S. *The World of Youthful Drug Use*. Berkeley: Regents of the University of California, 1967. (Mimeographed)

Brahen, L. S. "Housewife Drug Abuse." *Journal of Drug Education*, 3 (1973): 13–24.

Brecher, E. M. *Licit and Illicit Drugs*. Boston: Little Brown, 1972.

Broadhead, R. "Inundation of Family Life: The Impact of Professional Socialization on the Families of Medical Students." Los Angeles: University of California, 1978. (Mimeographed)

Brown, B. S., Gauvey, S. K., Myers, M. B., and Stark, S. D. "In Their Own Words: Addicts' Reasons for Initiating and Withdrawing from Heroin." *International Journal of the Addictions*, 6 (1971):635–645.

Brown, C. *Manchild in the Promised Land*. New York: Macmillan, 1965.

Burroughs, W. *Junkie*. New York: Ace Books, 1953.

Burt, M., Sowder, B., Glynn, T., and Yeldin, N. *An Investigation of Outcomes of Traditional Drug Treatment/Service Programs*. Bethesda, MD: Burt Associates, Inc., 1977.

Caplow, T. *The Sociology of Work*. New York: McGraw-Hill, 1954.

Carlson, K. "Treatment as Perceived by the Addict." *Addictive Diseases*, 2 (1976):569–584.

Cavan, S. *Hippies of the Haight*. St. Louis: New Critics Press, 1972.

Chambers, C. *An Assessment of Drug Use in the General Population*. New York: Narcotics Addiction Control Commission, 1971.

Chambers, C., Hinesley, R. K., and Moldstad, M. "Narcotic Addiction in Females: A Race Comparison." *International Journal of the Addictions*, 5 (1970):257.

Chambers, C., and Inciardi, J. "Physiological and Psychological Side Effects Reported during Maintenance Therapy." In C. Chambers and L. Brill

(Eds.), *Methadone: Experience and Issues*. New York: Behavioral Publications, 1973.

————. "Some Aspects of the Criminal Careers of Female Narcotics Addicts." Paper presented to the Southern Sociological Society, Miami Beach, FL, 1971. (Mimeographed)

Chein, I., Gerard, D. L., Lee, R. S., and Rosenfeld, E. *The Road to H*. New York: Basic Books, 1964.

Chessler, P. "Patient and Patriarch: Women in the Psychotherapeutic Relationship." In V. Gornick and B. Moran (Eds.), *Woman in Sexist Society*. New York: Basic Books, 1971.

Chinoy, E. *Automobile Workers and the American Dream*. Boston: Beacon Press, 1955.

Chodorow, N. "Being and Doing: A Cross-Cultural Examination of the Socialization of Males and Females." In V. Gornick and B. Moran (Eds.), *Woman in Sexist Society*. New York: Basic Books, 1971.

————. *The Reproduction of Mothering: Family Structure and Feminine Personality*. Berkeley: University of California Press, 1978.

Christenson, S., and Swanson, A. "Women and Drug Use: An Annotated Bibliography." *Journal of Psychedelic Drugs*, 6 (1974):4.

Climent, C. E. "Epidemiological Studies of Female Prisoners: Biological, Psychological, and Social Correlates of Drug Addiction." *International Journal of the Addictions*, 9 (1974):345.

Cloward, R., and Ohlin, L. *Delinquency and Opportunity*. New York: The Free Press, 1960.

Cohen, A. Y. "Inside What's Happening: Sociological, Psychological, and Spiritual Perspectives on the Contemporary Drug Scene." *American Journal of Public Health*, 59 (1969):2092–2095.

Colton, M. "Descriptive and Comparative Analysis of Self-perceptions and Attitudes of Heroin Addicted Women." In *Report on the Comparative Analyses of Psycho-social Variables: Self-perceptions and Attitudes, Social Support, and Family Backgrounds of Heroin Addicted Women*. Rockville, MD: NIDA, 1977.

Coombs, R., Fry, L. J., and Lewis, P. G. (Eds.). *Socialization in Drug Abuse*. Cambridge, MA: Schenkman Publishing Co., Inc., 1976.

Cooperstock, R. "Sex Differences in the Use of Mood-modifying Drugs: An Explanatory Model." *Journal of Health and Social Behavior*, 12 (1971): 238–244.

Cuskey, W. R. "Survey of Opiate Addiction among Females in the United States between 1850 and 1970." *Public Health Review*, 1 (1972):8–39.

Cuskey, W. R., Moffet, A. D., and Clifford, H. B. "A Comparison of Female Opiate Addicts Admitted to Lexington Hospital in 1961 and 1967." In C. Cohen, S. Roningson, and R. Smart (Eds.), *Psychotherapy and Drug Addiction I: Diagnosis and Treatment*. New York: MSS Information, 1974.

Cuskey, W. R., Berger, L., and Densen-Gerber, J. "Issues in the Treatment of Female Addiction: A Review and Critique of the Literature." *Contemporary Drug Problems*, 6 (1977):307–371.

Davis, N. "The Prostitute: Developing a Deviant Identity." In J. N. Henslin (Ed.), *Studies in the Sociology of Sex*. New York: Appleton Century Crofts, 1971.

DeLeon, G., and Wexler, H. K. "Heroin Addiction: Its Relation to Sexual Behavior and Sexual Experience." *Journal of Abnormal Psychology, 81* (1973):36–38.

DeLeon, G. "Phoenix House: Psychopathological Signs among Male and Female Drug-free Residents." *Addictive Diseases, 1* (1974):135.

Densen-Gerber, J., Weiner, M., and Hochstedler, R. "Sexual Behavior, Abortion, and Birth Control in Heroin Addicts: Legal and Psychiatric Considerations." *Contemporary Drug Problems, 1* (1972):783.

Dohner, V. A. "Motives for Drug Use: Adult and Adolescent." *Psychosomatics, 13* (1972):317–325.

d'Orban, P. T. "Heroin Dependency and Delinquency in Women—A Study of Heroin Addicts in Holloway Prison." *British Journal of the Addictions, 65* (1970):67.

Dupont, R. L. "Drugs, Alcoholism, and Women: Discrimination in Women's Drug Problems." Paper presented to the National Forum on Drugs, Alcoholism and Women, Miami Beach, FL, October 1975.

Duster, T. *The Legislation of Morality*. New York: The Free Press, 1970.

Ehrenrich, B., and English, D. *Complaints and Disorders: The Sexual Politics of Sickness*. Old Westbury, NY: The Feminist Press, 1973. (Glass Mountain Pamphlet, No. 2)

Eldred, C. A., and Washington, M. M. "Female Heroin Addicts in a City Treatment Program: The Forgotten Minority." *Psychiatry, 38* (1975):75.

Ellinwood, E. H., Smith, W. G., and Vaillant, G. E. "Narcotic Addiction in Males and Females: A Comparison." *International Journal of the Addictions, 1* (1966):33.

Feldman, D. J., and Feldman, H. S. "On the Etiology of Narcotic Addiction and its Relation to Curiosity." *Psychosomatics, 13* (1972):304–308.

Feldman, H. "Ideological Supports to Becoming and Remaining a Heroin Addict." *Journal of Health and Social Behavior, 9* (1968):131–139.

Fiddle, S. *Portraits from a Shooting Gallery*. New York: Harper and Row, 1967.

———. "Sequences in Addiction." *Addictive Diseases, 2* (1976):553–567.

File, K. N., McCahill, T. W., and Savitz, L. D. "Narcotics Involvements and Female Criminality." *Addictive Diseases, 1* (1974):177.

Finestone, H. "Cats, Kicks, and Color." In H. Becker (Ed.), *The Other Side*. New York: The Free Press, 1964.

Finnegan, L. P. "Narcotics Dependence in Pregnancy." *Journal of Psychedelic Drugs, 7* (July–Sept. 1975):3.

Finnegan, L. P., Connaughton, J. F., and Emich, J. P. "Comprehensive Care of the Pregnant Addict and Its Effect on Maternal and Infant Outcome." *Contemporary Drug Problems, 1* (1972):795.

Gaulden, E. C., Littlefield, D. C., Putoff, O. E., and Seivert, A. L. "Menstrual Abnormalities Associated with Heroin Addiction." *American Journal of Obstetrics and Gynecology, 90* (1964):155–160.

Gay, G., Newmeyer, J. A., and Winkler, J. J., "The Haight-Ashbury Free Clinic." In D. E. Smith and G. R. Gay (Eds.), *It's So Good, Don't Even Try It Once: Heroin in Perspective.* Englewood Cliffs, NJ: Prentice-Hall, 1972:71–85.

Gerstein, D., Judd, L. L., and Rovner, S. A. "Career Dynamics of Female Heroin Addicts." *American Journal of Drug and Alcohol Abuse, 6* (1977): 1–23.

Gioia, C., and Byrne, R. "Distinctive Problems of the Female Drug Addict: Experiences at IDAP." In E. Senay et al. (Eds.), *Developments in the Field of Drug Abuse.* Cambridge, MA: Schenkman, 1974.

Glaser, B. *Theoretical Sensitivity.* Mill Valley, CA: The Sociology Press, 1978.

Glaser, B., and Strauss, A. *The Discovery of Grounded Theory.* Chicago: Aldine, 1970.

Glaser, F. "Narcotic Addiction in the Pain-prone Female Patient." *International Journal of the Addictions, 1* (1966):2.

Goffman, E. *Asylums.* Garden City, NY: Doubleday, 1961.

———. *Stigma.* Englewood Cliffs, NJ: Prentice-Hall, 1963.

Goldman, A., and Schiller, L. *Ladies and Gentlemen, Lenny Bruce!* New York: Ballantine Books, 1975.

Goldstein, P. *Prostitution and Drugs.* Lexington, MA: Lexington Books, 1979.

Goode, E. *Deviant Behavior: An Interactionist Approach.* Englewood Cliffs, NJ: Prentice-Hall, 1978.

Gould, L. C., Walker, A. L., Lansing, E., and Lidz, C. *Connections: Notes from the Heroin World.* New Haven, CT: Yale University Press, 1974.

Haller, J. S., and Haller, R. M. *The Physician and Sexuality in Victorian America.* Urbana, IL: University of Illinois, 1971.

Hempden-Turner, R. *Sane Asylum: Inside the Delancy Street Foundation.* New York: William Morrow, 1976.

Hendler, H., and Stephens, R. "The Addict Odyssey: From Experimentation to Addiction." *International Journal of the Addictions, 12* (1977):25–42.

Hertz, R. "Addiction, Fertility, and Pregnancy." *Social Biology, 18* (1971): S40–S41.

Howard, J., and Borges, P. "Needle Sharing in the Haight: Social and Psychological Functions." *Journal of Health and Social Behavior, 11* (1970): 220–230.

Hughes, E. "Dilemmas and Contradictions of Status." *American Journal of Sociology, 50* (1945):353–359.

———. *Men and Their Work.* New York: The Free Press, 1958.

Hughes, H. M. (Ed.). *The Fantastic Lodge.* Greenwich, CT: Fawcett, 1961.

Hughes, P., Crawford, G. A., Barker, N. W., Schumann, S., and Jaffe, J. H. "The Social Structure of a Heroin Copping Community." *American Journal of Psychiatry, 128* (1971):551–558.

Inciardi, J. *Methadone Diversion: Experiences and Issues.* DHEW, Publication No. (ADH) 77–488, 1977.

Irwin, J. *The Felon.* Englewood Cliffs, NJ: Prentice-Hall, 1970.

————. "Participant Observation of Criminals." In J. Douglas (Ed.), *Research on Deviance*. New York: Random House, 1972.

————. *Scenes*. Beverly Hills, CA: Sage, 1977.

James, J. "Female Addiction and Criminal Involvement." Paper presented to the Pacific Sociological Association, Victoria, British Columbia, 1975. (Mimeographed)

————. "Prostitution and Addiction: An Interdisciplinary Approach." *Addictive Diseases*, 2 (1976):601–618.

Joe, G. W., Sensenig, J., Stocker, R. B., and Campbell, R. *An Evaluative Study of Methadone and Drug Free Therapies for Drug Addiction*. Texas Christian University, Fort Worth: Institute of Behavioral Research, 1971. (1 BR Technical Report No. 72–14)

Jones, M. *Beyond the Therapeutic Community*. New Haven, CT: Yale University Press, 1968.

Kanter, R. M. *Men and Women of the Corporation*. New York: Basic Books, 1977.

Kaubin, B. J. "Sexism Shades the Lives and Treatment of Female Addicts." *Contemporary Drug Problems*, 3 (1974):471.

Keeler, M. "Motivation for Marijuana Use: A Correlate of Adverse Reactions." *American Journal of Psychiatry*, 125 (1968):142–146.

Keniston, K. "Heads and Seekers: Drugs on Campus, Counterculture, and American Society." *The American Scholar*, 38 (1968):97–112.

Komarovsky, M. "Cultural Contradictions and Sex Roles." In A. Skolnick and J. Skolnick (Eds.), *Intimacy, Family, and Society*. Boston: Little Brown, 1974.

Krase, S. K. "Heroin Addiction among Pregnant Women and Their Newborn Babies." *American Journal of Obstetrics and Gynecology*, 75 (1958):754–758.

Larner, J., and Tefferteller, R. *The Addict in the Street*. New York: Grove Press, 1964.

Lemert, E. *Social Pathology*. New York: McGraw-Hill, 1951.

————. "Paranoia and the Dynamics of Exclusion." *Sociometry*, 25 (1962):2–20.

Lennane, K., and Lennane, R. "Alleged Psychogenic Disorders in Women— A Possible Manifestation of Sexual Prejudice?" *New England Journal of Medicine*, 288 (1973):288–292.

Lennard, H. *Mystification and Drug Misuses: Hazards in Using Psychoactive Drugs*. New York: Harper and Row, 1971.

Letkemann, P. *Crime as Work*. Englewood Cliffs, NJ: Prentice-Hall, 1973.

Levy, S. J., and Doyle, K. M. "Attitudes toward Women in a Drug Treatment Program." *Journal of Drug Issues*, 4 (1974):423–434.

Liebow, E. *Tally's Corner*. Boston: Little Brown, 1967.

Lindesmith, A. *Addiction and Opiates*. Chicago: Aldine, 1968.

Lindesmith, A., Strauss, A., and Denzin, N. *Social Psychology*. New York: Holt, Rinehart and Winston, 1977.

Linn, L. S., and Davis, M. S. "The Use of Psychotherapeutic Drugs by Middle-aged Women." *Journal of Health and Social Behavior*, 12 (1971):331–340.

Lofland, J. *Deviance and Identity*. Englewood Cliffs, NJ: Prentice-Hall, 1969.

Macro-Systems, Inc. *Three Year Follow-up of Clients Enrolled in Treatment Programs in New York City: Phase III*. Washington, D.C.: NIDA, 1975.

Marsh, J., and Neely, R. *Women Helping Women: The W. O. M. A. N. Center Evaluation Report: Year Three*. Rockville, MD: NIDA, 1976.

Matza, D. *Delinquency and Drift*. New York: John Wiley & Sons, Inc., 1964.

———. *Becoming Deviant*. Englewood Cliffs, NJ: Prentice-Hall, 1969.

McAuliff, W., and Gordon, R. "A Test of Lindesmith's Theory of Addiction: The Frequency of Euphoria among Long-term Addicts." *American Journal of Sociology*, 79 (1974):795–840.

Mead, G. H. *Mind, Self, and Society*. Chicago: University of Chicago Press, 1939.

Miller, G. *Odd Jobs: The World of Deviant Work*. Englewood Cliffs, NJ: Prentice-Hall, 1978.

Miller, J. S., et al. "Value Patterns of Drug Addicts as a Function of Race and Sex." *International Journal of the Addictions*, 8 (1973):4.

Mizner, G. L., Barker, J. T., and Werme, P. H. "Patterns of Drug Use among College Students: A Preliminary Report." *American Journal of Psychiatry*, 127 (1970):15–24.

Moore, M. *Buy and Bust: The Effective Regulation of an Illicit Market in Heroin*. Lexington, MA: Lexington Books, 1977.

Moore, W. "Occupational Socialization." In D. Goslin (Ed.), *Handbook of Socialization Theory and Research*. Chicago: Rand-McNally, 1969.

Mortimer, J., and Lorence, J. "Work Experience and Occupational Value Socialization: A Longitudinal Study." *American Journal of Sociology (Vol. 6)*. 84 (1979).

Murphy, S. "A Year with the Gangs of East Los Angeles." *Ms.*, 7 (July 1978).

Naeye, R. L., Blanc, W., Leblanc, W., and Khatamee, M. A. "Fetal Complications of Maternal Heroin Addiction: Abnormal Growth, Infection and Episodes of Stress." *Journal of Pediatrics*, 83 (1973):1055–1061.

Nash, G. "The Sociology of Phoenix House—A Therapeutic Community for the Resocialization of Narcotics Addicts." New York: Columbia University, 1969. (Mimeographed)

Nelkin, D. *Methadone Maintenance: A Technological Fix*. New York: George Braziller, 1973.

Newman, R. G. *Methadone Treatment in Narcotic Addiction*. New York: Academic Press, 1977.

Nurco, D. N. "Studying Addicts over Time: Methodology and Preliminary Findings." *American Journal of Drug and Alcohol Abuse*, 2 (1975):183–196.

O'Donnell, J. "Lifetime Patterns of Narcotic Addiction." In M. Roff and L. Robins (Eds.), *Life History Research in Psychopathology*. Minneapolis: University of Minnesota Press, 1972.

O'Donnell, J., Voss, H. L., Clayton, R. R., Slatin, G. T., and Room, R. G. *Young Men and Drugs: A Nationwide Survey*. Springfield, VA: National Technological Information Service, 1976.

Parry, H. J. "Patterns of Psychotropic Drug Use among American Adults." *Journal of Drug Issues*, 1 (1971):269–273.

Pelose, M. A., Frattorola, M., and Apuzzio, J. "Pregnancy Complicated by Heroin Addiction." *Obstetrics and Gynecology*, 45 (1975):512.

Perlmutter, J. F. "Drug Addiction in Pregnant Women." *American Journal of Obstetrics and Gynecology*, 99 (1967):569.

Ponsor, L., Soler, E., and Abod, J. "The ABC's of Drug Treatment for Women." Paper presented to the North American Congress on Alcoholism and Drug Abuse, San Francisco, 1974. (Mimeographed)

Prather, J., and Fidell, L. "Drug Use and Abuse among Women: An Overview." *International Journal of the Addictions*, 13 (1978):863–885.

Preble, E., and Casey, J. "Taking Care of Business: The Heroin User's Life on the Street." *International Journal of the Addictions*, 4 (1968):1–24.

Preble, E., and Miller, T. "Methadone, Wine and Welfare." In R. Weppner (Ed.), *Street Ethnography*. Beverly Hills, CA: Sage, 1977.

Ray, M. "The Cycle of Abstinence and Relapse among Heroin Addicts." *Social Problems*, 9 (1961):132–140.

Reichart, J., and Klein, R. (Producers). *An American Way of Dealing*. (Documentary) 1973.

Rementeria, J. L., Janakammal, S., and Hollander, M. "Multiple Births in Drug Addicted Women." *American Journal of Obstetrics and Gynecology*, 122 (1975):958.

Rementeria, J. L., and Nunag, N. N. "Narcotic Withdrawal in Pregnancy." *American Journal of Obstetrics and Gynecology*, 116 (1973):1052–1056.

Richards, L. "The Epidemiology of Youthful Drug Use." In F. R. Sarpitti and S. K. Datesman (Eds.), *Drugs and the Youth Culture* (Vol. 4). Beverly Hills, CA: Sage Annual Review of Drug and Alcohol Abuse, Forthcoming.

Robins, L. *Addict Careers*. Washington, D.C.: U.S. Government Printing Office, 1978. (U.S. Public Health Service Grants DA4RF 008 AA 03539 and 00013)

Rosenbaum, M. "Becoming Addicted: The Woman Addict," *Contemporary Drug Problems: A Law Quarterly*, 8 (Summer 1979):141–167.

———. "Difficulties in Taking Care of Business: Women Addicts as Mothers," *American Journal of Drug and Alcohol Abuse*, 6 (Fall 1979):431–446.

———. "The Heroin World: Risk, Chaos, and Inundation," *Urban Life: A Journal of Ethnographic Research* (Spring 1981):65–91.

———. "When Drugs Come into the Picture, Love Flies out the Window: Love Relationships among Women Addicts," *International Journal of the Addictions* (Forthcoming).

———. "Getting the Treatment: Recycling Women Addicts," *Journal of Psychoactive Drugs* (Forthcoming).

———. "Sex Roles among Deviants: The Woman Addict," 16, *International Journal of the Addictions* (Forthcoming).

Rosenbaum, M., and Rosenblum, B. "A History of the Concept of Career in Sociology." Paper presented to the American Sociological Association, Chicago, 1977. (Mimeographed)

Roth, J. *Timetables*. New York: Bobbs-Merrill, Inc., 1963.

Rothstein, P., and Gould, J. B. "Born with a Habit: Infants of Drug Addicted Mothers." *Pediatric Clinics of North America*, 21 (1974): 307–321.

Rubin, L. *Worlds of Pain: Life in the Working Class Family*. New York: Basic Books, 1976.

Rubington, E. "Drug Addiction as a Deviant Career." *International Journal of the Addictions*, 2 (1967): 2.

Ruzek, S. K. "Report to the California State Office of Narcotics and Drug Abuse Prevention and Treatment of Female Drug Dependency." 1974. (Mimeographed)

Sackman, B., Sackman, M. M., and DeAngelis, G. G. "Heroin Addiction as an Occupation: Traditional Addicts and Heroin Addicted Polydrug Users." *International Journal of the Addictions*, 13 (1978): 2.

Sagarin, E. *Deviance and Deviants*. New York: Praeger, 1975.

Scharse, R. "Cessation Patterns among Neophyte Heroin Users." *International Journal of the Addictions*, 1 (1966): 23–32.

Schatzman, L., and Strauss, A. *Field Research: Strategies for a Natural Sociology*. Englewood Cliffs, NJ: Prentice-Hall, 1973.

Schneck, H. "Narcotic Withdrawal Symptoms in the Newborn Infant Resulting from Maternal Addiction." *Journal of Pediatrics*, 52 (1958): 585.

Schultz, A. "Radical Feminism: A Treatment Modality for Addicted Women." In E. Seray, V. Shorty, and H. Alksne (Eds.), *Developments in the Field of Drug Abuse*. Cambridge, MA: Schenkman, 1975.

Schur, E. *Crimes without Victims*. Englewood Cliffs, NJ: Prentice-Hall, 1965.

Schutz, A. *Collected Papers, Vol. I*. M. Natanson (Ed.). The Hague, Netherlands: Martinus Mignoff, 1962.

Schwendiger, H. "The Insiders and the Outsiders: An Instrumental Theory of Delinquency." Ph.D. dissertation, University of California, 1963. (Mimeographed)

Seashore, M. J., Haberfeld, S., Leonard, D., and Irwin, J. *Prisoner Education: Project Newgate and Other College Programs*. New York: Praeger, 1976.

Shaw, H. *The Natural History of a Delinquent Career*. Chicago: University of Chicago Press, 1931.

Sheppard, C., Smith, D., and Gay, G. "The Changing Face of Heroin Addiction in the Haight-Ashbury." *International Journal of the Addictions*, 7 (1972): 122.

Slim, I. *Pimp: The Story of My Life*. Los Angeles: Holloway House, 1969.

Smith, D. M., and Gay, G. (Eds.) *It's So Good, Don't Even Try It Once*. Englewood Cliffs, NJ: Prentice-Hall, 1972

Smith-Rosenberg, C. "The Hysterical Women: Sex Roles in Nineteenth Century America." *Social Research*, 29 (Winter): 652–678.

Soler, E., Ponsor, L., and Abod, J. "Women in Treatment: Client Self-Report." In A. Bauman et al. (Eds.), *Women in Treatment: Issues and Approaches*. Arlington, VA: National Drug Abuse Center for Training and Resource Development, 1976.

Stoffer, S. S. "A Gynecologic Study of Drug Addicts." *American Journal of Obstetrics and Gynecology, 101* (1968):779.

Stone, M. L., Salerna, L. J., and Green, M. "Narcotic Addiction in Pregnancy." *American Journal of Obstetrics and Gynecology, 109* (1971):716.

Suffet, F., and Brotman, R. "Female Drug Use: Some Observations." *International Journal of the Addictions, 11* (1976):19–23.

Sutherland, E. *The Professional Thief.* Chicago: University of Chicago Press, 1937.

Sutter, A. "The World of the Righteous Dope Fiend." *Issues in Criminology, 2* (1966):177–182.

Tannenbaum, F. *Crime and the Community.* New York: Columbia University Press, 1938.

Terkel, S. *Working.* New York: Avon Books, 1974.

Terry, C. E., and Pellens, M. *The Opium Problem.* New York: The Haddon Craftsman, 1928.

Trocchi, A. *Cain's Book.* New York: Grove Press, 1960.

Vaillant, G. "The Natural History of Narcotic Drug Addiction." *Seminars in Psychiatry, 2* (1970):486–498.

Volkman, R., and Cressey, D. "Differential Association and the Rehabilitation of Drug Addicts." *American Journal of Sociology, 69* (1963):129–142.

Waldorf, D. *Careers in Dope.* Englewood Cliffs, NJ: Prentice-Hall, 1973.

Wallach, R. "Pregnancy and Menstrual Function in Narcotics Addicts Treated with Methadone." *American Journal of Obstetrics and Gynecology, 105* (1969):1226–1229.

Weissman, J. C., and File, K. N. "Criminal Behavior Patterns of Female Addicts: A Comparison of Findings in Two Cities." *International Journal of the Addictions, 11* (1976):6.

Weisstein, N. "Psychology Constructs the Female." In V. Gornick and B. Moran (Eds.), *Woman in Sexist Society.* New York: Basic Books, 1971.

Wellisch, D., Gay, G., and McEntee, R. "The Easy Rider Syndrome: A Pattern of Heterosexual and Homosexual Relationships in a Heroin Addict Population." *Journal of Family Proceedings, 9* (1970):425–430.

Wepman, D., Newman, R. B., and Binderman, M. *The Life: The Lore and Folk Poetry of the Black Hustler.* Philadelphia: University of Pennsylvania Press, 1976.

Weppner, R. "An Anthropological View of the Street Addict's World." *Human Organization, 32* (1973):111–121.

White, L. "It Isn't Easy Being Gay." In A. Bauman, et al. (Eds.), *Women in Treatment: Issues and Approaches.* Arlington, VA: National Drug Abuse Center for Training and Resource Development, 1976.

Williams, J. E., and Bates, W. M. "Some Characteristics of Female Narcotic Addicts." *International Journal of the Addictions, 5* (1970):245.

Winick, C. "Epidemiology of Narcotics Use." In D. M. Wilner and G. G. Kassebaum (Eds.), *Narcotics.* New York: McGraw-Hill, 1965.

———. "Some Aspects of Careers of Chronic Heroin Users." In E. Carroll

(Ed.), *Drug Use: Epidemiological and Sociological Approaches*. New York: John Wiley & Sons, Inc., 1974.

————. *Some Comments on Consequences of Chronic Opiate Use*. Washington, D.C.: U.S. Government Printing Office, 1977. (NIDA Monograph 16)

Wolfe, T. *Radical Chic and Mau-mauing the Flak Catchers*. New York: Bantam Books, 1972.

Yablonsky, L. *Synanon: The Tunnel Back*. New York: Macmillan, 1965.

————. *The Hippie Trip*. New York: Pegasus, 1968.

Zahn, M., and Ball, J. "Patterns and Causes of Drug Addiction among Puerto Rican Females." *Addictive Diseases*, 1 (1974): 203–214.

Zelson, C. "Infant of the Addicted Mother." *New England Journal of Medicine*, 288 (1973): 26.

Zinberg, N., and Harding, W. "The Effectiveness of the Sub-culture in Developing Rituals and Sanctions for Controlled Drug Use." In B. M. deToit (Ed.), *Drugs, Rituals and Altered States of Consciousness*. Rotterdam: A.A. Balkema, 1977.

Index